Sergey Brin, Larry Page, Eric Schmidt, and

Google

INTERNET BIOGRAPHIES™

Sergey Brin, Larry Page, Eric Schmidt, and
Google

CORONA BREZINA

ROSEN PUBLISHING®

New York

Published in 2013 by The Rosen Publishing Group, Inc.
29 East 21st Street, New York, NY 10010

Copyright © 2013 by The Rosen Publishing Group, Inc.

First Edition

Library of Congress Cataloging-in-Publication Data

Brezina, Corona.
Sergey Brin, Larry Page, Eric Schmidt, and Google/Corona
Brezina.—1st ed.
    p. cm.—(Internet biographies)
Includes bibliographical references and index.
ISBN 978-1-4488-6911-4 (library binding)
1. Google (Firm)—Juvenile literature. 2. Brin, Sergey, 1973—
Juvenile literature. 3. Page, Larry, 1973—Juvenile literature. 4.
Schmidt, Eric, 1955—Juvenile literature. 5. Internet industry—
United States—Juvenile literature. I. Title.
HD9696.8.U64G66344 2013
338.7'61025040922—dc23
                                                            2011039480

Manufactured in the United States of America

CPSIA Compliance Information: Batch #S12YA: For further information, contact Rosen Publishing, New York, New York,
at 1-800-237-9932.

Contents

INTRODUCTION /// 6

CHAPTER 1 THE FOUNDERS: SERGEY BRIN AND
LARRY PAGE ///////////////////////////////////// 10

CHAPTER 2 STANFORD AND SEARCH ENGINES ///// 21

CHAPTER 3 STARTING UP GOOGLE /////////////////// 34

CHAPTER 4 THE CEO: ERIC SCHMIDT //////////////// 49

CHAPTER 5 GOING PUBLIC ///////////////////////////// 60

CHAPTER 6 THE GROWTH OF GOOGLE //////////// 71

CHAPTER 7 CONTINUING INNOVATION ////////////// 88

FACT SHEET ON SERGEY BRIN, LARRY PAGE, AND
ERIC SCHMIDT ///////////////////////////// 99

FACT SHEET ON GOOGLE INC. //////////////////// 101

TIMELINE /// 102

GLOSSARY /// 105

FOR MORE INFORMATION ///////////////////////// 110

FOR FURTHER READING /////////////////////////// 117

BIBLIOGRAPHY ///////////////////////////////////// 121

INDEX /// 125

INTRODUCTION

On September 7, 1998, Google was officially incorporated. It was not an occasion of great fanfare. Its founders, Larry Page and Sergey Brin, had only recently rented a garage as headquarters. The pair had no business plan for making a profit. They had no interest in traditional marketing. They thought that somehow marketing would take care of itself. And they were right. Stories began to circulate about what could be found on the Internet using the Google search engine. People found jobs, long-lost relatives, answers to trivia challenges, and life-saving medical information.

A decade later, Google would be providing people with much more information distributed through many more products and services. Users could navigate by Google Maps, communicate through Google's Gmail e-mail service, stay informed with Google News, stay entertained with YouTube, and share their thoughts with the world through Blogger. A couple of years after that, a whole new realm of communication and mobile computing would be introduced with Google's Android platform for mobile devices.

One of the most attractive aspects of Google's business model is how much the company gives away for

Larry Page and Sergey Brin, Google's founders, pose in Mountain View, California, in 2002, when Google was still a small search engine company.

free. Looking at the range of products and services, it is almost tempting to wonder how Google manages to turn a profit, much less dominate as one of the nation's leading tech companies. The secret to Google's success is its phenomenally successful ad model. After Internet start-ups proliferated in the late 1990s, many of them folded, unable to translate innovative concepts into profitable strategies. Google survived and built on its ad revenues to thrive.

Google's official mission is "to organize the world's information and make it universally accessible and useful." The unofficial company motto is, "Don't be evil." The first core principle guiding Google's philosophy is, "Focus on the user and all else will follow." In a 2004 letter to potential investors, Page and Brin would open by warning them, "Google is not a conventional company. We do not intend to become one."

Google has retained its reputation for quirkiness. People often describe meeting Page or Brin wearing in-line skates as they went about their work running the company. Google's headquarters—the Googleplex—located in Mountain View, California, is sometimes described as a brilliant engineers' playground. Eric Schmidt was recruited as CEO in 2001 to provide "adult supervision" through his management expertise. Schmidt provided excellent guidance for the company, but he did not try to change its exuberant corporate culture.

Today, critics draw attention to a darker side of Google. In the course of its mission of organizing the world's information, Google has amassed a great deal of personal information about the people who use its services. Google's acquisition and use of this data raises privacy concerns. Google has also been accused of violating property rights, especially copyrights on published material. Google still stands by its motto of "Don't be evil," but today, this requires a great deal of trust from the people who use its products. Google has grown from an ambitious little start-up with the dream of changing the world into a global giant that really could—and has—changed the world.

CHAPTER 1

The Founders: Sergey Brin and Larry Page

The company that is now Google began as a partnership of ideas between two Stanford University graduate students with a shared vision. Although Sergey Brin was born in the Soviet Union and Larry Page came from the American Midwest, Google's two founders have much in common. Both Brin and Page had families that placed a high value on education and on intellectual curiosity. Both were encouraged early on in the interests that led them to computer science—computers for Page, mathematics for Brin. They both pursued higher education, which brought them to Stanford (located in Palo Alto, California). And eventually, they both had the confidence and nerve to set out on their own to start up a technology company together.

Brin is energetic and outgoing, and he is known for his sense of humor and informality. Larry is more reserved, occasionally prompting new acquaintances to wonder, "Does he talk?"

SERGEY BRIN

Sergey Mikhailovich Brin was born in Moscow, in what was then the Soviet Union, on August 21, 1973. He came from a family of scientists and intellectuals. One of his great-grandmothers had traveled to the United States to study microbiology at the University of Chicago. His paternal grandfather had been a mathematics professor. Both of his parents were accomplished mathematicians.

The Brins were dissatisfied with their lot in the Soviet Union, however, largely because of the discrimination they experienced due to anti-Semitism. Sergey's father,

A parade takes place in Moscow's central Red Square in 1975. Sergey Brin was born in Moscow. Until the fall of Communism in 1991, the Soviet regime strictly limited the personal freedoms of its citizens.

Mikhail, had dreamed of becoming an astronomer, but Jews were banned from studying physics at the university. He was also rejected for a Ph.D. program in mathematics because of anti-Semitic policies. Mikhail took a job working as an economist at the Soviet central planning agency and continued to study mathematics independently. He eventually earned his Ph.D. without formal enrollment in graduate school. Sergey's mother, Eugenia, worked for the research lab of the prestigious Oil and Gas Institute as a civil engineer.

In 1977, Mikhail attended a mathematics conference in Warsaw, Poland. The experience opened his eyes to the opportunities and freedoms that his international colleagues took for granted. Mikhail returned home determined to emigrate. Eugenia agreed to the plan, hoping for a brighter future for Sergey. When Mikhail applied for a visa to leave the Soviet Union, however, he was fired from his job. Eugenia had no choice but to quit her job, in case there were any counteraccusations. The Brins were not wealthy—they lived in a 350-square-foot (33-square-meter) apartment with Mikhail's mother—and they now faced financial hardship while their application was reviewed.

Finally, in 1979, the Brins' visa was approved. The family settled in Maryland, leaving most of their belongings behind. Mikhail—who changed his name to Michael— eventually secured a position as a math professor at the

University of Maryland. Eugenia became a research scientist at NASA's Goddard Space Flight Center. In 1987, Sergey's younger brother, Sam, was born.

Although Sergey emigrated at the age of six, his family's ordeals in the Soviet Union made a lasting impression on him. He cites an early fear of state authority with awakening his rebellious spirit. In 1990, Michael took a group of gifted high school math students, as well as his family, on a two-week summer exchange trip to the Soviet Union. On their second day in the bleak Soviet state, Sergey approached his father and sincerely thanked him for taking the family out of the Soviet Union. Later on, Sergey nearly got into trouble for impulsively throwing stones at a Soviet police car. To this day, as an adult, Sergey remains active in the Russian business community in the United States and retains his deep-seated opposition toward anti-Semitism and authoritarian regimes.

Upon their arrival in the United States, the Brins enrolled Sergey in the local Montessori school in Adelphi, Maryland. Sergey was still struggling to master English during his first year of school, but the Montessori program allowed him to pursue his interests in math and science. Later, Sergey would credit the Montessori school with fostering creativity. He also attended a Hebrew school for nearly three years, though his family was not actively religious. Sergey did not have a bar mitzvah, and he has not embraced traditional Jewish religious practices.

The popular Commodore 64 microcomputer was manufactured from 1982 to 1993. It featured 64 kilobytes of memory (RAM)—a primitively small figure by today's standards.

When Sergey was nine years old, Michael gave him his first computer, a Commodore 64. Sergey familiarized himself with the Internet and took up computer games, staying up late at night playing multi-user dungeons (MUDs) and writing his own game.

Sergey's teachers quickly recognized his mathematical abilities. He was a self-confident student who gained a reputation for correcting his teachers. Sergey attended Eleanor Roosevelt High School in Greenbelt, near Baltimore.

At this public school, he quickly outpaced the curriculum. He quit attending after three years and enrolled in the University of Maryland, in College Park, studying computer science and mathematics. Sergey excelled in college, completing several graduate-level classes during the course of his studies. He received his bachelor of science degree in 1993 after just three years. During summers, Sergey took jobs that allowed him to further explore his academic interests, including positions at Wolfram Research and General Electric Information Services.

After graduating, Sergey was awarded a graduate fellowship by the National Science Foundation. He enrolled in Stanford University in California to study computer science, with a particular interest in data mining—using computers to extract and analyze patterns from large fields of data. He quickly became known for his brilliance, passing all of his qualifying exams for his doctorate within a few months. Most students took three years to pass all of the exams. This fast track gave Sergey more time for new academic subjects, as well as extracurricular activities. He took up sailing, gymnastics, swimming, and rollerblading. He taught himself to cook. In 1995, he was awarded his master's degree in computer science, but he continued to work on his Ph.D.

Learning from Tesla

When Larry Page was growing up, one of his idols was the inventor and engineer Nikola Tesla (1856–1943). Tesla was a brilliant scientist but a very poor businessman. He never succeeded in commercializing his own inventions, although others were able to develop and profit from his ideas. Page was shocked that a brilliant innovator like Tesla could die penniless and unknown.

He took away a lesson from Tesla's story. He would not allow his innovations to be stolen and exploited. Even as he pursued his computer science degrees, he also studied business management. As he developed the precursor to the Google search engine at Stanford, he was protective of his concept and delayed publishing the details in an academic publication. As Page and Brin looked for early investors for their business, they remained secretive about their financial status and business model. Even after Google became wildly profitable, the founders concealed the extent of Google's success. Today, Google does not publicly disclose sensitive business information—not even empolyee salaries. Page and Brin are also intensely private about their personal lives and rarely give interviews to the press.

LARRY PAGE

Lawrence Edward Page—known today as Larry to almost everybody—was born on March 26, 1973, in East Lansing, Michigan. Although his parents were highly educated, Page retained a sense of connection to his working-class roots. His paternal grandfather worked in a factory for General Motors. He was active in the labor union and took part in the historic Flint Sit-Down Strike in 1937. In a 2009 commencement speech at the University of Michigan, Page recounted how his grandfather once drove his two children to Ann Arbor and announced that they were

Larry Page was born and grew up in East Lansing, Michigan, where his father taught computer science at Michigan State University, one of the top public research universities in the United States. A street near the campus is seen here in the mid-1970s.

going to go to college there. Both did indeed graduate from the University of Michigan.

Page's father, Carl, was afflicted with polio as a child and took more than a year to recover. Nevertheless, he became the first member of his family to graduate high school. He earned degrees in engineering and computer science, including a Ph.D., from the University of Michigan. Carl was a pioneer in the field of artificial intelligence. He spent most of his life teaching computer science at Michigan State University, in East Lansing, although he spent a year at Stanford in 1974–75. Page's parents had met at the University of Michigan and his mother, Gloria, held a master's degree in computer science. She taught computer programming at Michigan State University and later worked as a database consultant. His parents divorced when Larry was eight years old, and Carl eventually married a colleague at Michigan State. Still, both parents stayed involved in raising Larry. Although his mother is Jewish, Page has not adopted any formal religion.

Page has an older brother, Carl Jr., and a younger sister, Beverly. Nine years his elder, Carl also studied computer science at the University of Michigan. He was one of the founders of a technology company called eGroups. com, which was acquired by Yahoo! in 2000.

Unlike most children of his generation, Page began working with computers at a young age. The family acquired an early personal computer called the Exidy Sorcerer in

The Exidy Sorcerer, a home computer, was produced by an arcade game manufacturer from 1978 to 1980. The company packaged the shells of 8-track tapes (a music storage form) as cartridges housing computer circuit boards.

1978, and there were always science magazines and electrical engineering class assignments readily available around the house. Larry became the first student in his elementary school to turn in an assignment printed on a dot matrix printer. A few years later, when he was given a set of screwdrivers, he took apart his father's power tools.

Like Sergey, Larry attended a Montessori elementary school, located in Okemos. Unlike Sergey, he was a quiet student. Larry was also a talented saxophonist and, after his freshman year at East Lansing High School, was accepted into a summer program at the Interlochen Arts Academy. He graduated from high school in 1991.

Larry went on to study computer engineering at the University of Michigan. He'd already thought that some day he might start up his own company, and he took business courses during his undergraduate years and participated in a leadership development program called the LeaderShape Institute. He also served as the president of Eta Kappa Nu, the electrical and computer engineering honor society, and won the school's first Outstanding Student Award. Despite his academic achievements, one of Larry's proudest feats at the University of Michigan was building a functional inkjet printer with a Lego brick casing. He received his bachelor's degree in 1995, graduating with honors.

He headed west to Stanford for graduate school, nervous despite his strong academic record. He once told a University of Michigan alumni magazine, "At first, it was pretty scary. I kept complaining to my friends that I was going to get sent home on the bus." In 1996, during his first year at Stanford, his father died at the age of fifty-eight of complications from pneumonia. He was devastated.

He earned his master's degree in computer science but remained at Stanford to continue working on his Ph.D.

Chapter 2

Stanford and Search Engines

L arry Page and Sergey Brin first met in the spring of 1995. Page had traveled to Stanford for a weekend visit for prospective students. Brin, who had already been studying at Stanford for two years, was giving a group tour of nearby San Francisco. By some accounts, each initially found the other obnoxious. But they talked and argued all weekend and discovered that, in terms of intellect and wide-ranging curiosity, they clicked.

Stanford University is renowned as one of the premier high-tech institutions of learning in the United States. The school encourages entrepreneurship and innovation among its students and even aids in the process of obtaining patents for graduate students with entrepreneurial ambitions. Silicon Valley, the home base for many important technology companies, emerged in southern California around Stanford. Corporations such as Hewlett-Packard, Yahoo!, and Sun Microsystems had their

Stanford University's William Gates Computer Science Building, completed in 1996, contains state-of-the-art teleclassrooms, computer labs, computer history exhibits, and workspace for 550 faculty, staff members, and students.

roots at Stanford. Bill Gates, the cofounder of Microsoft, recognized the school's contributions to the tech world, even though he never attended the university. Gates gave millions of dollars to Stanford toward the construction of a new center for computer science. In 1996, Page and Brin, the rest of the computer science department, and the computer systems laboratory moved into the newly opened William Gates Computer Science Building.

In Stanford's graduate computer science department, students worked closely with faculty members on cutting-edge projects. In the mid-1990s, the exciting technological frontier was the new World Wide Web. Computer users were just beginning to use the Internet for research, social interactions, and commerce. Individual sites were just starting to be linked together in a huge interconnected network. At this time, the National Science Foundation established a program called the Digital Library Initiative. Brin and Page were among the students who worked on projects for the program.

DOWNLOADING THE INTERNET

When Page arrived at Stanford, he picked as his adviser Terry Winograd, a specialist in the new field of human-computer interaction (HCI). Winograd was dazzled by the scope of vision his student exhibited. In *Googled*, author Ken Auletta describes how Page would unexpectedly bring up outlandish notions such as "doing something with space tethers or solar kites." Page shared an office in the new Gates building with four other graduate students. Brin also spent a lot of time in the crowded jungle of the office, and people began to refer to the two of them as a unit: "LarryandSergey."

One of Page's early priorities was the selection of his doctoral thesis. He had grown up in a family full of college professors, and he considered it possible that he might someday pursue an academic, rather than an entrepreneurial, career. A Ph.D. doctoral thesis topic can have a lasting impact on a candidate's future career. Page considered a number of ideas, but he found that the new World Wide Web particularly captured his interest.

The Web was growing quickly, but there was not yet an easy way to navigate the maze of sites. Users could hunt for information with a new tool called a search engine—some of the first were HotBot, Lycos, Excite, and Inktomi. These early search engines often did not yield useful results, however. Pages were not listed in any logical order, and a user might have to scan through dozens of useless

David Filo and Jerry Yang cofounded the Internet corporation Yahoo! in 1994. Like Brin and Page, they were both Stanford students when they conceived of the core idea behind their tech company.

entries before finding a relevant site. The new company Yahoo!—founded by two Stanford alumni—took a different approach. It employed editors to categorize sites into a directory. But Yahoo! could not keep pace with the expanding Internet.

In investigating different search engines, Page noticed an interesting feature of the AltaVista service. In addition to listing a Web site, AltaVista listed sites that linked to that site. Page pointed this out to one of his advisers, Hector Garcia-Molina, and they spent time seeing which computer science pages drew the most links.

AltaVista did not utilize this information in its search engine. Page realized, though, that analyzing these links could provide useful results. To explore the subject further, he would need an extensive database of links to work with. Page approached Winograd and announced that he was going to download the Web onto his computer. He thought that it would take a couple of weeks.

DEVELOPING PAGERANK

Meanwhile, Brin was also trawling the Internet in the course of working on his own project. Along with his adviser, Rajeev Motwani, he was data mining the contents of Web sites and searching for trends in the information assembled. For this, he had to write a program for a Web crawler that would "crawl" the Internet for links and other data. Because Page's and Brin's areas of interest overlapped, Brin was easily persuaded to join Page in the work of gathering and analyzing Web links. Brin eagerly attacked the mathematical and programming challenges of the project.

Page was basing his work on the premise that the number of links to a site corresponded with that site's importance. Each incoming link for a specific site was, in essence, a vote in popularity or a confirmation that it was a useful site. Page concluded that Web sites could be ranked according to the number of links pointing to them. This rank could be used to organize the results yielded by a search engine. The most popular sites would be weighted toward the front of the list.

It took Page a lot longer than two weeks to download the link structure of the Internet. Brin tackled the complicated mathematical problem of tracking the links to each site, as well as the links associated with each linking site. As the project grew, it required huge amounts of computer capacity on Stanford's system and extensive hardware and equipment. Page and Brin frequently badgered the computer science department to grant them more resources. On one occasion, they brought down Stanford's computer network. They also strung computers together in their dorm rooms. Brin, a talented hardware engineer, bought cheap disk drives for storage space and made them work more quickly by

A photo of Larry Page and Sergey Brin is reflected in the glass exhibit case for the original Google storage server cased in Lego blocks, which is on display at the Stanford School of Engineering.

modifying the terminals. Later, Google would continue this trend of frugality and innovation in designing its own hardware infrastructure. Page called his ranking algorithm PageRank, naming it after himself.

Early on, Page and Brin had no plans for establishing their own search engine. But as they immersed themselves in the Web, they realized that PageRank could be applied to searches. It could potentially yield much more useful results than commercial search engines. Page called the first version of his project BackRub because it worked by looking backward at the links that pointed to sites. They ran their first test in March 1996, starting a Web crawl at Stanford's site. The crawler located sites that linked to Stanford and moved on to find sites that linked to those linking sites. It was a success. By August, BackRub was working well enough that Page and Brin made it public on Stanford's Web site.

Page and Brin quickly realized that the number of linking sites was not the only factor that determined a site's value. The prominence of the originating page was also important. A technology magazine site and a personal Web site might both include links to Stanford, but the link from the tech site was more valuable. PageRank could determine which linking sites were prominent by looking backward again and finding that more sites linked to the tech site than the personal site. On this basis, the tech site would be given a higher rank. Giving a higher value to important, well-trafficked sites made PageRank's rankings more relevant.

As the Web grew, there would be more links between sites, and there would be more data for PageRank to apply to search results. This asset gave BackRub an advantage over commercial search engines, most of which tended to give more and more irrelevant answers as the number of results grew.

GOOGLE AT STANFORD

Increasingly, Page and Brin were feeling torn between the commercial possibilities of their project and their academic pursuits. They could start their own company, but that would require putting their Ph.D. programs on hold. An alternative was to license BackRub to an established company. Or they could continue to explore the academic aspect of the project. BackRub was so huge and complex that it had become notorious in the computer science department, where it used up considerable resources. People were beginning to ask when Page and Brin were going to publish their results. Page, however, was reluctant to reveal too many details, wary that someone else in the competitive tech world might infringe on possible future trade secrets.

It was also true that BackRub was still in development, and its creators preferred hands-on work to writing up a paper. In 1997, they decided that it needed a more marketable name. Someone suggested "googol," the term for 1^{100}—the numeral one with a hundred zeros behind it. Page promptly registered google.com as a domain name. They soon realized that they had misspelled it, but googol.com had already been taken. And Page liked the sound of "google." Stanford began hosting the search engine at google.stanford.edu. Brin designed the Google homepage, with its white background and multicolored letters.

A Profitable Patent

Because Page and Brin were student employees at Stanford when they developed PageRank, Stanford legally owned the invention. Stanford operates an Office of Technology Licensing (OTL) that promotes the development of intellectual property. The OTL helps guide inventors such as Page and Brin through the complicated process of receiving a patent for their idea. Any eventual royalties from the patent are shared by Stanford and the inventor.

Initially, Page, Brin, and the OTL tried to license the patent to PageRank to an existing company, but nobody would meet their price. When they started up Google, Page and Brin made an arrangement with Stanford to hold exclusive licensing rights for PageRank. In return, the school received 1.8 million shares of stock. When Google eventually went public in 2004, these shares were immensely valuable. Stanford immediately sold about 10 percent of its stake, making $15.7 million, and sold the rest in 2005 for a total of $336 million.

In 1997, Page and Brin began trying to interest existing search engine companies in licensing their search engine. They negotiated with Excite's founders, pitching Google as a means of increasing both traffic and revenue. On one occasion, they proposed a comparison match between Google and Excite's own search engine. Google yielded much more accurate results. The Excite executive then claimed that Google's results were actually too good for business. If users got their information immediately, they would spend less time on Excite's search page. This way of thinking was directly opposite to Page and Brin's own philosophy. As a company, one of Google's top priorities would be providing users with a positive experience in using its technology. The deal with Excite did not go through.

Page and Brin also met with one of the designers of AltaVista, who was intrigued by the concept. Executives at AltaVista's parent company, however, refused to make an offer. They preferred to rely on ideas developed within AltaVista, rather than incorporating ideas from outsiders. Yahoo! also declined to adopt the Google system.

In 1998, Page and Brin finally published a paper on their search engine. They presented "The Anatomy of a Large-Scale Hypertextual Web Search Engine" at a conference in Australia. The paper was well received, but Page and Brin wanted more than academic recognition. They believed that they had a potentially great product based on a groundbreaking concept. They wanted to see it reach the public. They still did not want to postpone their Ph.D.s, and their families were ambivalent about them leaving their studies. Nonetheless, they began exploring the logistics of starting their own company.

The first issue was money. But they were in the heart of Silicon Valley. For two brilliant Stanford computer whizzes who had the backing of many well-respected faculty members, finding investors was not a huge problem. One of their professors, David Cheriton, recommended that they contact Andy Bechtolsheim, founder of Sun Microsystems. Bechtolsheim suggested an informal meeting, and they all met on Cheriton's porch the next morning. Bechtolsheim was intrigued by their idea and

Before he became an investor in Google, Andy Bechtolsheim in 1982 cofounded the computer company Sun Microsystems, based on a project he had worked on as a graduate student at Stanford.

impressed with their confidence. He immediately wrote out a check to Google, Inc., for $100,000, despite the fact that Page and Brin did not yet have a bank account. Other investors—including Jeff Bezos, founder of Amazon.com—also agreed to back Google. In total, Page and Brin raised $1 million to start up their company.

They officially filed for incorporation on September 4, 1998. They prepared to move out of Stanford, taking a leave of absence. Prior to leaving, they gave a last talk about their Google project before faculty and students. Many of these colleagues had helped Page and Brin during the creation of PageRank, BackRub, and the original Google. This was their chance to explain their accomplishments and describe their dreams and goals for their new company. Page and Brin related the technical details behind their search engine. They discussed their strategies to make Google a commercial success, but they also talked of their hopes of changing the world.

CHAPTER 3

Starting Up Google

Like many tech start-ups, Google set up business in a garage. Page and Brin rented the garage—as well as a few rooms in the house—from Susan Wojcicki, who was then a manager at Intel. Their new headquarters were in Menlo Park, not far from Stanford. Page was the official chief executive officer (CEO) of the company. Brin was president. They hired their first employee, fellow Stanford student Craig Silverstein, and an office manager.

Google did not stay in the garage for long. In early 1999, the company moved to offices in downtown Palo Alto, and, as Google grew, it occupied several other locations before finally establishing its permanent headquarters at the Googleplex in Mountain View in 2004. But many aspects of Google's corporate culture—prevalent attitudes and practices—extend back to the cramped, hectic early days in the garage. There was not enough room for everyone to have private workspaces. Today, Google strongly encourages employees to work collaboratively and express

Google's first headquarters was a garage belonging to Susan Wojcicki, who appreciated the free cable and interesting company provided by the Googlers. Google later bought the house where the company first set up business.

their opinions and ideas freely. The early Google team got used to having access to a kitchen and other conveniences of someone's home. Today, Google is acclaimed for the amenities it provides employees.

KEEPING UP WITH THE SEARCH

Google attracted its initial investors because of the innovative idea behind its search engine. Even after Page and Brin struck out on their own, the search engine remained

Google's Competitors

Even as Google has grown and evolved, the company has gained more and more competitors in industries beyond Silicon Valley. Early on, Google's competitors were other search engines, such as Inktomi, AltaVista, and Excite. Though Google once partnered with Yahoo! to provide search services, the deal ended after a couple of years. Yahoo! soon set out to develop its own search engine, putting it in competition with Google. Microsoft also began offering its own search service.

Once Google moved beyond offering search services, it acquired new rivals with every development. Its ad programs put it in competition with GoTo (later renamed Overture). Its Web browser, Google Chrome, put it in competition with Microsoft in another arena. Android, Google's operating system for smartphones, was a challenge to Apple's iPhone. Google introduced its social network, Google+, in response to Facebook's dominance.

In addition, Google's hosting of content puts pressure on many traditional media industries. Book and magazine publishers, movie studios, and television networks all feel threatened by Google's success in its mission "to organize the world's information and make it universally accessible and useful."

in beta form—a test version—for a period. Now they had to transform that idea into a product that could make a profit. Google came into existence during a tech boom, when investors and ordinary computer users alike were beginning to see great potential in the expanding Internet. But many start-ups failed to prosper because their founders were unable to figure out a way to make money off of promising concepts.

Early on, Google managed about one hundred thousand searches every day. In late 1998, *PC Magazine* listed Google in its list of top 100 Web Sites and Search Engines. Salon.com profiled Google in glowing terms: "Amazing— a search engine that actually works." The article pointed out that on most search engines, a search for "President Clinton" might not even yield the White House in the first ten results. This was because the search function typically scanned pages for keywords. If the phrase "President Clinton" was not featured prominently on the White House home page, the site might be overlooked. Google also targeted keywords for its searches. Because of PageRank, however, useful sites would rise to the top of the list, rather than less relevant pages with a frequent occurrence of the phrase "President Clinton." By early 1999, Google was handling five hundred thousand searches per day. Investors had been drawn by the founders' bold ideas, but Web users were gravitating to Google because of its effectiveness.

The first priority at Google was improving its search engine. Even after Page and Brin removed the "beta" label, maintaining the search engine was a constant challenge. The Web was growing, and their base of users was increasing. Google had to invest in more and more computers and hardware to keep up. At first, five computers were enough to crawl the Web for links. By the end of 1999, the number had grown to eighty, out of thousands of computers that Google used to keep its search engine running.

In the "Our Philosophy" section on Google's Web site, the first item states, "Focus on the user and all else will follow." From the beginning, Google's commitment to optimizing the user's experience was a concrete objective, not an empty motto.

Early on, one of the engineers at Google realized that analyzing users' searches could enable Google to refine its results. Google keeps a log of all the searches performed on its search engine. If you perform a Google search, Google tracks your entries. It knows whether you click on one of the results or you instead refine your queries. Google knows your geographical location.

By examining search patterns, Google's engineers could identify areas for improvement. They took interpretive signals into account—people searching for "hot dogs" would get results about food, not pets. They built in a spell-check function so that users would not have to perform multiple searches to hit on the correct spelling.

They fine-tuned their name detection function so that the search engine would recognize personal names, even those that overlapped with common words, such as "Brown" or "Cook." Many people don't realize the numerous functions built into the search box. It works as a calculator and unit converter. Adding words such as "weather," "define," and "map" will yield a relevant response featured above the Web search results. These functions were added to yield fast, convenient information on popular search queries. For users with a Google account, Google personalizes search results based on past search history.

Another problem that Google engineers tackled early on was search spam—irrelevant junk results, much of it

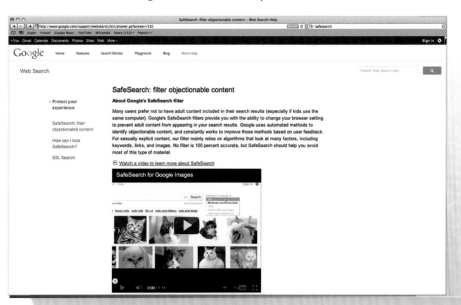

This is Google's Web page offering information about its SafeSearch filter (http://www.google.com/support/websearch/bin/answer.py?answer=510). Filtering out offensive content from its search results has been a priority and an ongoing challenge for Google from its earliest days. Many innocent searches can yield inappropriate results unrelated to the search terms entered.

consisting of advertisements. In 1999, they developed a filter called SafeSearch that prevented inappropriate material from being listed in the results. They also began countering certain search engine optimization (SEO) methods, in which sites attempted to artificially boost their ranking. Common methods included repetitions of certain keywords or using "link farms" to raise the number of links to a site. Google frequently tweaks its algorithms to eliminate search spam.

In early 2000, Google's search engine experienced a crisis. The Web crawlers constantly trawled the Internet and stored data on an index. For a couple of months, though, the index was not updated because of frequent server failures. Search engine users would receive out-of-date results. In the fast-paced tech world, this was a huge problem. Google fixed the problem by substantially improving its infrastructure and file system. Google engineers also rewrote parts of the code, improving search accuracy. Numerous revisions have followed, usually without public fanfare.

Moreover, despite the success of its search engine, Google has continued to devise innovative ways to improve its performance. In 2011, Google Instant was incorporated as a search feature. As soon as the user begins entering a query, Google generates predictive search terms and results that are refined as the user continues typing. Also in 2011, Google introduced significant changes to its search algorithms intended to make results more current.

HIRING THE BEST

When Google moved out of the garage where it had first started up business, the company had eight employees. By mid-1999, there were thirty-five employees and the company had to move once again to a larger space. Their new site was a 42,000-square-foot (3,902-sq-m) building in Mountain View, not far from Palo Alto.

Google was quickly building up a world-class team of talented engineers and computer scientists. From the beginning, Page and Brin aimed to recruit people with a mind-set akin to their own. They wanted their hires to be "Googley," a term that reflects Google's corporate culture. They would be brilliant, resourceful, ambitious, and idealistic. They would not be bound by conventional business or management attitudes. Computer scientists and engineers, above everyone else, were royalty at Google. The engineers were the ones whose concepts and projects enabled Google to become a superpower among tech companies. Personnel in management, marketing, sales, and other nontechnical areas learned that they would succeed better if they took an engineering, data-driven approach to doing their jobs.

Early Googler Marissa Mayer eventually rose to become vice president of location and local services, charged with making connections with local businesses. Here, she announces the launch of Google Instant in 2010.

But how could a small start-up with no clear plan for turning a profit attract top talent in the highly competitive environment of Silicon Valley? Today, Google is renowned for its workplace perks. Back then, Google employees worked off of doors set on sawhorses instead of desks. To save money on storage and processing, they bought dozens of cheap computers at a time and assumed that a couple would fail every day. But many engineers were eager to work for a company that would give them the opportunity to pursue bold and innovative projects. Even as some

The Google Doodle

In the fall of 1999, Brin had the idea of tweaking Google's logo for Halloween, replacing the "o"s with two pumpkins. He was excited about Halloween, and so were Google users. The pumpkin version of the logo was hugely popular.

This was the beginning of Google Doodles, Google's practice of modifying the logo on Google's search homepage for holidays and other noteworthy occasions. Google Doodles occasionally mark the birthdays of important figures, anniversaries of historic events, and current events such as the Olympics. Clicking on the logo generally yields search results for the subject of the Doodle, but some Doodles are interactive. The Google Doodle for May 21, 2010, celebrated the thirtieth birthday of the Pac-Man arcade game with a playable version of the logo. A study estimated that users around the globe spent 4.8 million hours playing Google's Pac-Man logo!

Some Doodles appear globally on all of Google's search domains. Others, such as Doodles marking national holidays, are featured only in specific countries or regions.

companies were cutting back on research, Google encouraged research that could lead to breakthroughs. Many early hires first learned about Google from other engineers who were impressed by Page and Brin's vision and savvy.

For seasoned engineers who had worked for large companies, joining Google was a risk. The risk—and their hard work—paid off, though, because early hires received stock options that eventually made them millionaires. Marissa Mayer, an engineer with a degree from Stanford, was an early Google employee. Urs Hölzle, accompanied by his huge dog, Yoshka, arrived to transform Google's infrastructure. A young biology major named Salar Kamangar asked to be taken on as a volunteer, and Page and Brin added him to the payroll. Susan Wojcicki, whose garage first housed Google, was hired as marketing manager. Mayer, Hölzle, Kamangar, and Wojcicki eventually became top executives at Google. Another early

employee was Krishna Bharat, a computer scientist with

extensive experience working with search engines. He eventually conceived of the project that would become Google News. Dr. Jim Reese, a brain surgeon, joined Google as operations chief, managing the hardware infra-structure. A doctoral candidate named Matt Cutts moved

Google designer Ryan Germick tweaks a Google Doodle honoring Brazilian artist Tarsila do Amaral's 125th birthday. Some Google Doodles even feature animated videos.

from North Carolina to California to tackle the problem of search spam. He often unofficially engages the public about Google's products and policies, and he offers general Internet tips.

Even in the early days, Brin and Page were highly selective in their hiring. Candidates underwent multiple interviews with several of their potential coworkers, and Brin and Page met with every candidate personally. Today, Google's hiring practices are notoriously rigorous. Many promising candidates attend eight interviews total. Recruiters assemble a file on candidates between twenty and forty pages long. Every potential recruit is discussed and analyzed by a hiring council. The application is then sent to the executive level, with Page making the final decision. The whole process lasts up to two months, and less than one half of 1 percent of applicants are offered the job.

BETTING ON GOOGLE

Page and Brin succeeded in putting together a team of brilliant engineers and creating a great search engine, but they still were not making a profit. Also, as they invested in equipment and hired more employees, the initial million-dollar start-up investment began to run out. In early 1999, Page and Brin assigned Kamangar the task of drawing up a business plan and pitching Google to venture capitalists.

They also hired a sales executive, Omar Kordestani, who had previously worked for Netscape.

Venture capitalists provide funds to start-ups in return for a stake in the company. During the late 1990s, venture capital companies were booming and investing heavily in Internet technology. Page and Brin needed to find a source of funding, but they did not want to relinquish any control over Google. They decided to pursue two different prestigious firms, Kleiner Perkins Caufield & Byers and Sequoia Capital, to split the venture capitalists' stake in the company.

Representatives from both companies were impressed by Google's presentation. John Doerr of Kleiner Perkins, an astute businessman and computer engineer, was particularly struck by Page's confidence in Google's potential. When asked how big he expected Google to grow, Page responded, "ten billion" in revenue, despite the fact that Google was not profitable and had no clear business plan. Mike Moritz of Sequoia, a former journalist, was also struck by their entrepreneurial spirit, but he also had a more practical consideration in backing Google. Sequoia had funded Yahoo!, and Moritz saw Google as a valuable potential business partner for Yahoo!.

Both Doerr and Moritz agreed to invest in Google, but they refused to share the deal. Page and Brin decided that in that case, they would decline the offers and look for funding elsewhere. The two venture capital companies withdrew their objections and agreed to split the investment. Doerr and Moritz did, however, attach certain conditions to their support. Their primary demand was that Google hire an experienced CEO to manage the business.

On June 7, 1999, in Google's first press conference, Page and Brin announced that Kleiner Perkins and Sequoia were investing $25 million in Google. The deal kindled considerable interest in the tech world. The investment was a huge amount of money to grant to a young company, and it was very rare for two major venture capital firms to work cooperatively.

Soon afterward, Google achieved another triumph. Later that June, Google negotiated a deal to supply the search function for Netscape, which had just been acquired by America Online (AOL). On the first day, Google's servers could not handle the traffic from both the Netscape and Google search sites. Google shut down its own site until it could acquire more computers—a move that demonstrated its integrity in honoring its business commitments.

In the summer of 1999, Terry Winograd received a query about Page's office space at Stanford, still occupied by Page. Page and Brin both returned to the university and finally cleared out their offices, making their departure from Stanford seem even more final.

CHAPTER 4

The CEO: Eric Schmidt

By 2001, Google was the leading search engine on the Web. People were starting to use the word "google" as a synonym for "search." (The word "google" officially entered the *Oxford English Dictionary* in 2006.) The company went global in its reach, offering its search engine in twenty-six languages. Google survived the bursting of the dot-com bubble, which caused many tech start-ups to go out of business or merge with established companies.

Now that they were partnered with venture capitalists, Page and Brin were under intense pressure to devise a realistic business plan. They envisioned their revenue coming from three sources: ad sales, a hardware search device, and fees for licensing their search technology. In mid-2000, Google finalized its biggest licensing deal when it agreed to provide search technology to Yahoo!. Google beat out one of its competitors, Inktomi, who had previously provided Yahoo's search service. At this time, Yahoo! was one of the giants of the Internet. When Google's search engine took over, users quickly noticed an improvement in the search, and traffic to Yahoo!'s site increased. This benefited Google because Yahoo!'s page featured the Google logo. Millions of Internet users were introduced to Google through this partnership with Yahoo!.

Nonetheless, the Yahoo! deal did not secure Google's fortunes, and Google still lacked a clear plan for making a profit. Google's venture capital backers were not upset about the company's lack of earnings. But John Doerr and Mike Moritz were exasperated that Page and Brin had not yet hired a CEO, as promised during the venture capital deal. It was not unusual for young companies to take on "adult supervision," the term used for professional managers experienced in running a business. Page and Brin, though, were reluctant to cede control to an outsider. At one point, the two founders proposed that they continue managing Google on their own. Doerr and Moritz rejected the suggestion. As Page and Brin continued to stall, Doerr had the idea of demonstrating firsthand how a quality CEO could benefit a company. He arranged for them to meet with some of the most revered tech CEOs in Silicon Valley. After talking to Steve Jobs of Apple, among others, Page and Brin agreed to start a search for a CEO.

Even so, they began the search with little enthusiasm. They were still suspicious of the notion of a corporate outsider taking over their company. The search process dragged on for eighteen months, with Brin and Page rejecting more than a dozen candidates. Finally, Doerr arranged for Eric Schmidt to visit Google's headquarters.

MEET ERIC SCHMIDT

At first, Schmidt had little interest in joining a scrappy start-up company like Google. He had already established a successful career working for a number of prominent Silicon Valley companies, finally becoming CEO of the network software company Novell in Provo, Utah. Leaving to become Google's CEO would be a huge gamble.

Eric Schmidt brought a broad level of management experience to Google. During his fourteen years at Sun Microsystems, he worked his way up the corporate ladder while the company itself prospered.

Eric Emerson Schmidt was born on April 27, 1955, in Falls Church, Virginia, near Washington, D.C. His father, Wilson Schmidt, was an economics professor who worked at the U.S. Department of the Treasury during President Richard Nixon's administration. His mother, Eleanor, had

Brin, Schmidt, and Page entertain themselves during a break while attending a sales conference. Schmidt's business expertise proved a good match to Google's instinct for innovation.

received a master's degree in psychology. Eric Schmidt had two brothers. He grew up in Blacksburg, Virginia, and graduated from Yorktown High School in Yorktown, Virginia, in 1972. He first began working with computers in high school, using machines called time-share

computers that were programmed with punch cards. Multiple users shared each machine, and they were linked by telephone lines. Savvy computer users like Schmidt worked at night when the telephone lines were less busy.

Schmidt attended Princeton University in New Jersey and received a bachelor of science degree in electrical engineering in 1976. During summers, he worked at Bell Labs, which was then a renowned research and development facility. Schmidt went on to study computer science at the University of California, Berkeley, and earn an M.S. degree and a Ph.D. in 1982. He worked summers at Xerox PARC and joined the research staff at PARC after receiving his degree. PARC was a prestigious lab that invented many technologies used in computing today, and Schmidt worked with pioneers in software development.

The Google Philosophy

In 2001, as Google was on the verge of developing AdWords and attaining profitability, a group of Google employees gathered together to draft a set of corporate values. The final list combined practical, idealistic, and whimsical points:

1. Focus on the user and all else will follow.
2. It's best to do one thing really, really well.
3. Fast is better than slow.
4. Democracy on the Web works.
5. You don't need to be at your desk to need an answer.
6. You can make money without doing evil.
7. There's always more information out there.
8. The need for information crosses all borders.
9. You can be serious without a suit.
10. Great just isn't good enough.
(Source: http://www.google.com/about/corporate/company/tenthings.html)

Above any of the others, the sixth point, summarized as "Don't be evil," came to embody Google's ruling principle. It quickly became a catchphrase around the office and, later, was featured in the founders' IPO letter when Google went public. Today, however, the phrase "Don't be evil" is sometimes redirected back to Google as a protest against some of the company's controversial business practices.

In 1983, Schmidt joined Sun Microsystems, where he stayed for fourteen years, working in both engineering and management roles. His wife, Wendy, who he had married in graduate school, also worked at Sun. (The couple had two sons.) Schmidt led the team that developed the programming language Java, and he rose to the position of president of Sun Technology Enterprises. In 1997, he left to become CEO of Novell. Schmidt continues to teach strategic management part-time at Stanford Business School.

Schmidt was a friend of Doerr's, and in 2000, Doerr suggested that Schmidt consider a management role at Google. After much urging, Schmidt agreed to meet with Page and Brin. He did not realize that he was being considered for CEO. Rather than a traditional interview, Schmidt found himself in a vigorous debate, much of it consisting of Page and Brin's criticism of his performance at Novell. Nonetheless, the pair were impressed by Schmidt. He was an accomplished engineer, as well as an experienced executive. Schmidt also seemed to appreciate Google's vision.

Schmidt officially became Google's CEO in March 2001. Page became the president of products, and Brin took the position of president of technology. Soon after Schmidt's arrival, the three made an informal pact that they would all stick with Google for twenty years.

ADS AND PROFITABILITY

Schmidt arrived during a low point in Google's fortunes. Despite the $25 million injection of capital, money was again threatening to run out. Google's investors were beginning to get anxious, especially in the aftermath of the dot-com bubble burst. But Google was about to find the key to profitability and previously unimagined growth.

Early on, Page and Brin were not interested in focusing on advertising. Many search engines mixed paid advertisements in with search results. Page and Brin refused to follow this practice, believing that it was

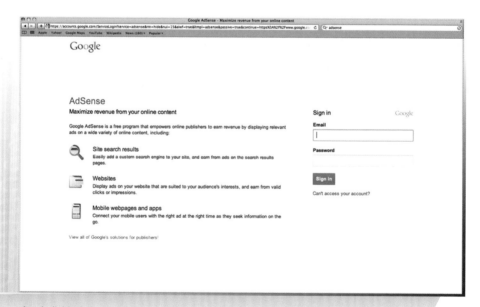

Any individual or organization that hosts content on the Internet can make money by displaying ads with Google's AdSense (http://www.google.com/adsense). Google also profits from the arrangement.

deceptive to the user. They also rejected distracting and obtrusive forms of advertising, such as flashing banner ads or pop-up ads. In 1999, Google introduced its first ad system: text-only block ads that were matched to search keywords. Ads were positioned to the right of search results and labeled clearly as "sponsored links." Ad sales, including an early large-scale test with the online bookstore Amazon.com, failed to earn much money.

Engineers analyzed advertising strategies to find ways they could improve on conventional approaches. Instead of having a sales team pitch ads directly to advertisers, Google introduced a self-service system. Anybody could buy a Google ad linked to a keyword that would be featured to the right of the search results. But Google wanted users to see ads that they might actually find useful, not just the most expensive ads. Therefore, ads that received more clicks—a higher click-through rate—rose to a higher position. This indicated which ads were most popular to users. Both users and advertisers were satisfied with the ads that were displayed. Google's system, dubbed AdWords, debuted in October 2000.

Engineers continued to tweak the ad system. One major improvement was based on the ad model of GoTo, later renamed Overture, a rival search engine. Most companies charged advertisers a certain amount each time the page was viewed, whether the user clicked on the ad or not. GoTo devised a system where the advertiser was charged only when the user clicked on the ad. Therefore, the advertiser would only have to pay if the ad was effective.

Google adopted the pay-per-click feature, as well as another GoTo innovation: an auction system for ads. Potential advertisers had to make a bid to have their ad linked to a particular keyword. Google adopted this practice, but Google engineers modified GoTo's system. Instead of paying the highest bid, the winning bidder would pay only a penny more than the second-highest bid. Therefore, the winner would not have to worry about overpaying for a winning bid.

A third new function regulated the quality of ads. Each ad was assigned a quality score, based largely on the click-through rate. The quality score of the potential ads, along with the contenders' bids, would determine the ranking of ads displayed on a page. Google had figured out a way to encourage relevant ads on its site, and users responded.

The combination of these three features—the pay per click, the second-bid auction, and the quality regulation—created a fantastically lucrative advertising model. The system launched as a test called AdWords Select in January 2002. It was such a success that Google quickly discontinued the original version of AdWords.

Google engineers next looked for a means of expanding its ad system. If Google could link ads to keywords on the search result page, why couldn't it do the same for text on any Web page? Google engineers developed a program that would extract keywords from Web pages. Owners of Web sites could register with Google to carry Google ads, their content determined by the keywords on the page and generated automatically by algorithms. The owners would split advertising profits with Google. The program, called AdSense, debuted in 2003. Google ads could now expand across the entire Internet.

CHAPTER 5

Going Public

G oogle was firmly established as the world's dominant search engine. In mid-2001, it announced that it had indexed a billion URLs. By the end of the year, that number had grown to three billion. Also, in mid-2001, Google introduced Image Search, its first specialized search option. Others, such as Google Product Search, Google Scholar, and Google Videos, later followed.

Schmidt settled into his new job at Google. Many employees were relieved by the indications that the company would be adopting a more coherent management structure. Schmidt also demonstrated that he understood the corporate culture at Google. Shortly after his arrival, engineer Amit Patel—one of Google's earliest handful of employees—observed that Schmidt had his own office. Patel was sharing an office with four others. Schmidt, upon being asked, agreed to share his office with Patel. The arrangement continued for about six months.

Conflicts did arise, however, between Schmidt and Google's founders. Page and Brin objected to measures that they believed made the company too bureaucratic. Because the trio controlled the company jointly, they had to learn to function as a team. Doerr recruited the help of Bill Campbell, a former head football coach at Columbia University who had executive experience at many Silicon Valley companies. Campbell met regularly with Page, Brin, and Schmidt, as well as Doerr and Moritz. He listened to everyone's concerns and negotiated solutions agreeable to all.

In early 2002, Schmidt found himself in opposition to Brin and Page concerning Google's biggest potential deal in its history. AOL, then an Internet powerhouse, proposed that Google become its search engine provider. If Google won the contract, it would beat out its competitors Inktomi and Overture. Page and Brin wanted to pursue the deal aggressively. Schmidt considered it too risky. AOL demanded a huge financial guarantee, and Schmidt argued that the terms could ruin Google if they lost money as a result. Google's investors, however, sided with Page and Brin, and Google began powering AOL's search engine and sharing the ad revenue. The deal was profitable for both companies. Subsequent arrangements with Internet companies such as Earthlink and Ask Jeeves followed.

One of Google's earliest services had its roots in a Google engineer's reaction to the terrorist attacks

A Googler relaxes in a nap pod at the Googleplex in Mountain View, California. In addition to receiving generous perks, Google employees are reportedly the highest paid in the IT industry.

of September 11, 2001. During the aftermath, Krishna Bharat found himself obsessively scouring the Web for updated news stories from various sites. It occurred to him that it would be convenient to have links to all of the available news sources accessible on one page. This would also give users a broader range of perspectives than what they might otherwise experience. Bharat developed a news search engine that automatically assembled links to the day's top stories, drawing on thousands of sources. Google News was unveiled in late 2002. Bharat assumed that media industries would welcome the increased Web traffic brought by Google's exposure. Instead, some news organizations objected to Google's use of their content on the Google News site. It was the first major instance when public debate arose out of Google overstepping boundaries in its business policies and practices.

With the launch of Google News, the company had begun to branch out from its original focus on search and ads. This fit with Google's official mission "to organize the world's information and make it universally accessible and useful." In 2002, though, few people in the world anticipated how far Google would extend its mission.

MOVING INTO THE GOOGLEPLEX

As Google prospered, the company outgrew its facilities and began searching for a new space. Google found its ideal headquarters at the former complex of Silicon Graphics, Inc. (SGI), a software company that could no longer afford its lavish building with its innovative design. The site consisted of four buildings providing about 500,000 square feet (46,452 sq m) of workspace. Google took over the "Googleplex," as the Mountain View headquarters was dubbed, in early 2004. Google has since bought more land surrounding the campus, and the campus now includes more than twenty buildings. Today, Google owns or leases more than 4 million square feet (371,612 sq m) of office space.

Gmail

On April 1, 2004, Google introduced Gmail, its e-mail service. The new system offered an unbelievable 1 gigabyte of storage (the amount has since been increased). Also, it provided e-mail search capabilities superior to that of its rivals.

The first public reaction was one of confusion. Google was notorious for its April Fool's Day pranks. Was Gmail a real service or just a joke? The next response was suspicion and outrage over privacy concerns. This was because Google used AdSense to run targeted ads in Gmail. People did not react well to the idea that Google was scanning their e-mail, even though the process was automated. To Google engineers, this was no different from routine scanning of e-mail for spam or viruses, a common practice of many e-mail services. And while Gmail included ads, it did not share personal information with advertisers. Nonetheless, privacy advocates denounced Google. A California congresswoman even introduced short-lived legislation aimed at banning ads in e-mail.

The outrage died down, but mistrust of Google's privacy policies never completely subsided. The public was now aware of the enormous amount of personal information that Google collected and stored on its servers.

Visitors to the Googleplex are impressed by features such as the *Tyrannosaurus rex* model skeleton on the main campus, the replica of Richard Branson's *SpaceShipOne* installed in one of the main buildings, and the real-time projection in lobbies of search queries from around the world. The Googleplex offers generous recreation facilities, including mini swimming pools, volleyball courts, and award-winning cafeterias. The design features and decorations are both quirky and environmentally friendly. There are giant lava lamps inside, as well as solar panels on some roofs.

Workspaces are designed to foster creativity and collaboration. Instead of working inside individual cubicles, Google employees are clustered together at workstations. Google discourages wasted space and believes that high human density in the workplace encourages interactions between coworkers.

GOOGLE'S INITIAL PUBLIC OFFERING (IPO)

To outsiders, it was clear that Google was thriving. The company now had more than 1,500 employees who enjoyed lavish perks at Google's huge new corporate campus. New offices were being opened across the United States and internationally. Google search services and ads had become universal. Google was beginning to acquire smaller companies, such as the parent company of Blogger. It introduced Google Local, a feature that was later folded into the popular Google Maps service.

But outsiders had no specific details on Google's profitability. This was a deliberate strategy on the part of the founders and Schmidt to conceal the magnitude of Google's financial success. If their stunning earnings were made public, it would bring unwelcome attention from competitors. Google's leaders preferred to remain quiet on the particulars about the company's operations for as long as possible. But that was going to have to change.

In 2004, Google finally announced that it was going to go public—instead of remaining privately held, Google's shares would be publicly traded on the stock market. When a company goes public, it issues an initial public offering (IPO), which is the first chance for the public to buy its stock. In the business world, an IPO of a big company like Google is a major event. Unlike private companies, publicly traded companies can raise money by issuing more stock. Google would never again have to turn to private investors for capital.

Nonetheless, neither Page nor Brin were eager to take Google public. This would mean being held accountable to shareholders and thus relinquishing some degree of control. It would also require that they disclose more of their financial information. But they had little choice. Going public would enable their venture capitalist back-

On August 19, 2004, Schmidt (*second from left*) and Page (*center*) attend a ceremony in New York City as Google Inc. is formally listed on the NASDAQ stock exchange for the first time.

ers to finally reap a return on their gamble. In addition, they would have had to disclose financial numbers anyway because of their high level of assets and number of shareholders.

Going public would make Page and Brin billionaires because of the stock they held in Google. Hundreds of Google employees would instantly become millionaires.

Usually, the IPO process is handled by investment bankers. The bankers set an opening price, often somewhat undervalued. They then allocate the first shares to banking insiders, who quickly resell these shares at a higher price. Characteristically, Page and Brin rejected the established procedure. They approached the IPO as if it were an engineering problem and chose to offer their IPO as a "Dutch auction." This would make the initial stock sales available to the general public. The founders also ensured that they would remain in control of the company by making "Class B" stock held by Google's inner circle worth more votes per share than "Class A" stock sold to investors.

On April 1, Google finally presented its financial information to a group of bankers. Google's chief financial officer displayed a slideshow to a group of bankers that tracked solid profits. Then, in the tradition of April Fool's Day, he confessed that those were the wrong numbers and unveiled the real balance sheet. Google's profits surpassed anyone's expectations, exceeding $300 million up to that point.

To the financial world, and somewhat to the general public, Google's IPO process quickly turned into a three-ring circus. Page and Brin proved to be difficult clients for investment banks interested in handling the auction. They refused to comply with the usual fees involved in the process. They didn't take advice from experienced financiers and attached rigorous conditions to various aspects of the deal. They scorned the traditional "road show," in which company leaders attended private sessions with investors.

Their behavior at these meetings left potential backers dissatisfied and offended.

Later in April, Google filed its S1, the Security and Exchange Commission (SEC) pre-IPO document. Usually, the S1 is a dry statement outlining financial strengths and risks. But Brin and Page included a controversial Founder's Letter, titled "'An Owner's Manual' for Google Shareholders." It began, "Google is not a conventional company. We do not intend to become one." They also cited the unofficial motto, *"Don't be evil.* We believe strongly that in the long term, we will be better served—as shareholders and in all other ways—by a company that does good things for the world even if we forgo some short term gains." The SEC demanded revisions to the letter, such as clarifications to statements like "making the world a better place." Page and Brin did not comply.

Wall Street bankers were unhappy with Google's methods. Financial reporters in the media were unclear about Google's future prospects. Google's missteps did not increase confidence in the company. The low point of the process occurred during the "quiet period" before the IPO, when media contact was prohibited for Google. Shortly before the auction was to begin, a well-known magazine released an interview with Page and Brin that had been conducted before the start of the quiet period. Its publication violated the SEC's rules and caused a public relations disaster for Google. For the IPO to continue, the entire interview was inserted into the S1.

With all the bad publicity, Google reduced its projected price range and the number of shares offered. The IPO took place on August 19, 2004. Schmidt and Page traveled to New York for the event. Brin went to work at the Googleplex as usual. Stock shares went out for $85 apiece and jumped to $100.01 by the end of the day, giving Google a market value of $27 billion. It was an impressive result, though smaller than the earliest projections. From there, stock values rose, proving doubters wrong. Five years later, each share was worth about $450, and Google's total value, about $140 billion.

After the IPO, Schmidt acknowledged that Google had made mistakes in the process. But the publicity surrounding the event kept Google's name in the news, which brought more traffic to Google's site.

CHAPTER 6

The Growth of Google

In the Founder's Letter included in Google's 2004 IPO document, Larry Page informed potential investors: "Our goal is to develop services that significantly improve the lives of as many people as possible. In pursuing this goal, we may do things that we believe have a positive impact on the world, even if the near term financial returns are not obvious." Nevertheless, Google's business strategy produced impressive profits year after year.

Page and Brin continued to issue an annual Founder's Letter, and these highlighted Google's growth as well as its commitment to following the "Don't be evil" mantra in making important decisions. In 2006, Brin wrote about Google's acquisition of YouTube, but he also wrote about the creation of Google.org, Google's philanthropic initiative. The 2008 Founder's Letter marked Google's tenth anniversary. It mentioned the new Chrome Web browser and discussed advances in the

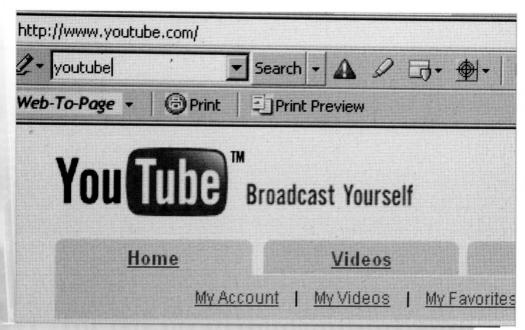

In 2006, Google acquired YouTube. YouTube (http://www.youtube.com) is a free service, but users must log in to their Google accounts to use some features, such as leaving comments or uploading videos.

Android mobile platform, as well as expressing pride in "the small role Google has played in the democratization of information." It also reflected on Google's earliest days, when "the search index sat on a small number of disk drives enclosed within Lego-like blocks." Every letter included a progress report on search and ad functions, which remained Google's core focus.

The triumvirate arrangement of leadership, with Page, Brin, and Schmidt running the company collaboratively, proved a success. Page and Brin tended to focus

Google's April Fool's Mentality

At Google, April Fool's Day is the most anticipated holiday of the year. The company has a long tradition of April Fool's pranks, both internal and public. The first external April Fool's joke, staged in 2000, was "MentalPlex," the mind-reading search engine. On April 1, 2004, it announced that the Google Copernicus Center was hiring for a research center on the moon. In 2007, Google introduced Gmail Paper, through which users could request paper versions of their e-mails with huge ads printed on the back in red ink. April Fool's Day in 2007 also saw the launch of TiSP, the Toilet Internet Service Provider. YouTube also celebrates April Fool's Day. In 2009, it revealed that users get better reception if the video image is flipped upside down. In 2011, Google changed its name to Topeka.

Google's playful attitude sometimes extends to its business dealings. When Google was preparing for its IPO in 2004, the company announced that it would sell shares worth $2,718,281,828. Those are the opening ten digits of the mathematical constant e, making Google's price a joke that only mathematicians would immediately catch.

on Google's internal workings while Schmidt represented Google's public face to the world. Schmidt, however, has raised controversy with some of his offhand remarks, especially concerning privacy. He famously stated during a 2009 interview with the TV business news channel CNBC, "If you have something that you don't want anyone to know, maybe you shouldn't be doing it in the first place."

THE GOOGLERS

The first Founder's Letter also mentioned: "Our employees, who have named themselves Googlers, are everything … We hope to recruit many more in the future. We will reward and treat them well." Google did indeed became famous for its generous employee perks. In 2007—the first year Google was eligible for consideration—*Fortune Magazine* named Google the #1 best company to work for. It has remained in the top ten on the list ever since.

Google encourages a relaxed workplace atmosphere, but the selectivity of its hiring guarantees that its ambitious employees do not shirk their duties. The company believes that the expenses are justified because satisfied employees, free of distractions, are more productive. Googlers have access to generous recreational amenities, a masseuse, on-site doctors, laundry facilities, a car wash, and on-site haircuts. The Googleplex boasts high-tech toilets with heated seats. Exercise balls and bicycles are freely available in various places for employee use. Googlers can bring their dogs to work. Google actively recruits young college graduates, and coming to work at the Googleplex is an easy transition from a college campus. In addition, Google is generous with more conventional benefits, such as insurance, time off (for vacations, sick days, and maternity or paternity leave), and savings plans.

One of the most famous Google perks is the free gourmet food available to all employees. According to Susan Wojcicki, the practice began when Google oper-

Numerous cafés and food kiosks located in the Googleplex provide employees with meals free of charge. Googlers can choose from a variety of cuisines that emphasize healthy and organic ingredients.

ated out of her garage and had available a fridge full of food. Even before moving to the current Googleplex, Google hired Charlie Ayers as company chef. Ayers, who had occasionally cooked for the American rock band Grateful Dead, had replied to an ad with the inducement, "The only chef job with stock options!" (as quoted by Steven Levy in *In the Plex*).Today's Googleplex includes more than a dozen cafés where Googlers can eat their meals free of charge, as well as snack rooms where free food is available at any time.

A long-established tradition at Google is Friday afternoon TGIF. It began as an informal gathering of Google employees, a cross between an information session and an office party. Page and Brin would always attend. "Nooglers"—new Google employees—are officially introduced at TGIF. By the time Google had grown from a handful of employees to thousands, TGIF had become more structured. The TGIF session would be webcast to Googlers across the country and the world. The high point of TGIFs is the question-and-answer session, in which any employee could submit questions, with no restrictions, to Page and Brin.

Another well-known Google policy is the "20 percent rule." Googlers spend 20 percent of their time working on independent projects. This means of encouraging innovation set Google apart from typical corporations, where managers disapprove of wasting time on side projects.

Googlers' 20 percent projects often yield results that contribute to official Google products—for example, Krishna Bharat's early development of Google News was a 20 percent project. The 20 percent rule is also attractive to potential employees interested in working for a company where they can conduct independent research.

BRANCHING OUT

When Google issued its IPO in 2004, most of its products and services were directly involved with search and advertisement. Gmail had been an exception. After going public, though, Google began branching out from its original focus. It began offering a variety of new products and services, from maps to a word processing program.

Google also began increasing its acquisition of smaller companies. From 2001 to 2004, Google acquired fourteen smaller companies. In 2005 alone, it acquired ten companies, many of them related to mobile software, a new area of focus for Google. In 2010, Google acquired more than two dozen smaller companies. DowJones VentureSource, a research firm, ranked Google the year's top acquirer of venture-backed companies. Google's acquisitions were also getting bigger and more expensive. Most of these acquisitions have been integrated into existing Google products and services. For example, in 2010, Google announced the $700 million acquisition of the travel and airline software

Most of Google's Street View 360-degree images are captured by specialized cameras mounted on cars. Here, in Israel, a Google Street View tricycle prepares to photograph Jerusalem's narrow Old City alleyways, which are inaccessible to cars.

company ITA. In 2011, it unveiled Google Flight Search, a search engine tool that uses ITA's technology to make online travel searches easy, enabling travelers to shop for flights by date, destination, price, and time span of flight.

Today, Google's Web site lists dozens of products in seven different categories. The first item under "Web" is Google's well-recognized search engine. Another item in this category is Google Chrome, Google's Web browser.

Google began developing Chrome in 2006 and released it in 2008, even though some within the company were wary of competing directly with Microsoft's Internet Explorer browser. They were also reluctant to create a rivalry with Mozilla, the developer of Firefox and a former partner. Chrome was innovative in that it functioned as a platform for running Web-based applications. In this way, Chrome anticipated a trend toward cloud computing, in which applications and data are stored on remote servers, rather than on devices such as individual desktop computers. Users access applications and data over a network. For cloud computing to be user-friendly, Web browsers have to be fast. Google engineers concentrated on optimizing Chrome's speed in running Web applications. After Chrome's release, its competitors all made their browsers run faster, a reaction welcomed by Google.

The next category, Mobile, features a gallery of the different mobile devices that support Google's Android operating system, one of Google's most ambitious new areas of development. It also includes a selection of applications (apps) that can be used in multiple platforms.

The Media category offers features related to videos, images, books, and news. This includes the popular site YouTube and the controversial Google Books, which was at the center of a lengthy court battle.

The Geo section includes Google Maps, introduced in 2005. The map service allows users to view custom maps as a street grid or from a satellite view. Google Maps offers driving directions and shows information on local businesses. One of the features of Google Maps, Street View, triggered an international controversy over privacy issues. Street View allows users to view the surroundings at street level through continuous photographs that simulate the experience of driving through and looking around. When Street View debuted in 2007, there was

Visitors check out Android products at a trade show. In 2011, Google announced software called Google Wallet, which allows users to pay for purchases with a tap of the phone on a terminal.

a public outcry over identifiable faces and license plates on vehicles. Privacy advocates objected to Google posting images of people engaged in activities that they would not want publicized. Google engineers were taken by surprise—after all, the images were taken in public spaces, so the company was not engaged in anything illegal. Nevertheless, Google quietly implemented a policy of blurring faces and license plates. Google Earth, another feature in Geo, allows users to see satellite imagery, terrain, and buildings in 3-D.

The Home and Office section includes a variety of practical and convenient features such as Gmail, a calendar, and a language translation function. One of the tools available is Google Docs, a free Web-based application introduced in 2006. Users can create, store, and share documents, spreadsheets, and presentations. Google Docs is a cloud computing service that stores data on Google's servers and does not require software. Google introduced an off-line version in 2011, a move intended to make Google Docs more competitive with Microsoft Office.

The final three categories are Social, which includes blogs and group interaction tools; Specialized Search, which covers various areas such as patent searches, financial information, and alerts for e-mail updates; and Innovation, which mostly provides tools for programmers.

TELEVISION AND TELEPHONES

As digital communication became faster and grew to include media of a variety of forms, Google moved beyond the printed word. In 2005, it debuted Google Video to mediocre reviews—the service did not even play videos online. Around the same time, three young engineers launched a site called YouTube where users could upload videos. It quickly became sensationally popular.

Instead of trying to compete with YouTube, Google bought the young company in 2006. It paid $1.65 billion, by far the largest sum for any acquisition up to that point. Google continued to allow YouTube considerable independence. It kept its own offices separate from the Googleplex. In 2010, however, longtime Googler Salar Kamangar replaced one of the YouTube founders as CEO.

YouTube brought Google a new array of legal difficulties because the site hosted copyrighted content as well as personal videos. YouTube's policies prompted threats of lawsuits from major media companies and led to prolonged negotiations. In 2007, the media company Viacom sued Google for copyright infringement. The courts ruled in Google's favor in 2010.

Google has also faced criticism for its regulation of YouTube content. Some criticize Google for failing to screen videos adequately. Others criticize Google for overreaching censorship in removing videos, especially those with polarizing political content.

Another sphere of expansion for Google was in mobile devices. The market for smartphones and other online mobile devices was surging. In 2005, Google acquired a mobile software company called Android. Google wanted to make the Android operating system a reliable platform for running software applications. Instead of being limited to a specific type of hardware, it would run on multiple networks. It would also create another niche for Google's ads.

In 2007, Google lobbied the Federal Communications Commission (FCC) to keep a certain share of airwave spectrum space open. This accessibility would mean that telecommunications giants owning the space could not block Google's applications on their network. The FCC agreed.

With its development of Android, Google became a competitor of Apple, the creator of the iPhone. Before this point, Google and Apple had had a good working relationship, and Page and Brin had been friends with Apple's CEO Steve Jobs.

The first phone running the Android platform was unveiled in late 2007. Further partnerships followed, and many of Google's products and services have been made available as Android apps.

GOOGLE BOOK SEARCH

Google Book Search—introduced in 2003 as Google Print and later renamed Google Books—began with the founders' dream of creating an online library where anyone could access any book ever written. Page believed that Google could make that dream a reality. Brin was also enthusiastic about the scheme. Schmidt supported the project for a different reason. Online books would provide Google with more content and traffic that could be targeted by Google ads. Opponents of Google Book Search would later bring up this very point.

Brin began experimenting with a hand-operated book scanner in 2002. Eventually, Google engineers devised robotic scanners that could digitize books. In 2004, Google announced that it was partnering with some of the greatest university and public libraries in the world to digitize their collections.

The announcement sparked controversy because the project included scanning books under copyright, in which case the authors still owned the rights to the book. In 2005, authors and publishers sued Google over the digitization of copyrighted books. Google's lawyers argued that Google was not violating copyright laws because even though Google scanned entire books, it only made snippets of a book available to the public. Page and Brin were especially passionate about making "orphan books" more accessible. Orphan books, those that are still under copyright but are out of print, make up about 75 percent of all copyrighted books. In a *New York Times* op-ed article defending Google Print Search, Brin wrote, "With rare exceptions, one can buy [books] only for the small number of years they are in print. After that, they are found only in a vanishing number of libraries and used bookstores."

In 2008, a settlement was reached. It was a complicated plan in which Google would create a database of out-of-print books. Google would also provide libraries with computer terminals on which the public could read entire books. In addition, people could buy digital versions from Google, with the author receiving a portion of the payment.

But the settlement still had to be approved in court. After the terms were announced, there was a torrent of protest directed at Google. The settlement would make Google the only seller of most of the books published in the twentieth century. Hundreds of influential people and groups publicly objected to the settlement, including some former supporters of Google Book Search. Ominously, the objectors included the U.S. Department of Justice (DOJ), which regarded the settlement to be anticompetitive. In early 2011, a judge rejected the settlement, stating that it gave Google a near monopoly. The decision throws Google's effort to digitize millions of books from libraries into legal limbo.

GOOGLE IN CHINA

Google expanded internationally as it grew into a major technology company. Today, Google has well over a hundred domains for its search engine. For example, a Google user in France uses the domain google.fr. As Google's presence has grown across the world, the company has opened offices and expanded its hardware infrastructure overseas.

China had the potential to be an important market for Google. The country, with a population of more than a billion people, was growing in prosperity and industrialization. There were more Internet users in China than in the United States.

Google introduced its Chinese search page, at google.cn, in 2006. Search results were subject to censorship laws by the Chinese government. The government blocked much information on the Tiananmen Square protests of 1989, for example, and on the Tibetan independence movement. Google was uncomfortable with the censorship demands but accepted that a level of compliance was necessary to do business in China at all. Brin, who had emigrated from a repressive regime, was particularly troubled by the situation.

In 2008, when China hosted the summer Olympics, its censorship demands intensified. The Chinese government even wanted Google to censor the Chinese language results at google.com. At a company meeting, Brin expressed dissatisfaction with Google's China policies. Then in late 2009, hackers broke into Google's system and stole information from the Gmail accounts of Chinese human rights activists. The attacks were traced to China. In early January 2010, at Brin's urging, Google announced that it would stop censoring the Chinese search engine. If Google could not reach an arrangement with the Chinese government, it would shut down google.cn.

The Chinese government refused to yield, and the Chinese search engine closed down. Instead, users were referred to the Hong Kong Google search engine, which did not censor results. Google continued to maintain some products and services in China, such as Google Maps. Google's presence in China diminished drastically because of the discontinuation of google.cn.

CHAPTER 7

Continuing Innovation

In January 2011, Google announced that Larry Page was going to assume again the job of CEO in April 2011. After a decade at Google's helm, Eric Schmidt would step aside to take the position of executive chairman. Sergey Brin would take the title "cofounder" and concentrate on strategic projects. Page, in addition to his duties as CEO, would steer product development and technology strategy.

Schmidt would later post on Twitter, "Day-to-day adult supervision no longer required!" He expanded his thoughts on the Google official company blog in a post accompanied by a photo of Schmidt, Brin, and Page posing by Google's self-driving car, one of the company's side projects. Page is sitting in the driver's seat. Brin, in turn, praised Schmidt in the 2010 Founder's Letter, saying, "It's hard to think of anyone on the planet who could have done a better job than Eric has."

Page and Brin make a "No hands!" gesture from inside one of Google's self-driving cars while Schmidt stands by. The car is guided by GPS and sensors that allow the car to "see" its surroundings.

The announcement came on the same day that Google released its financial results for the fourth quarter of 2010 and the entire fiscal year. The news was positive. Google had earned nearly $30 billion in revenue in 2010. Revenues for the fourth quarter of 2010 had increased 26 percent over the 2009 figures.

"THE BOYS HAVE GROWN UP"

In a 2008 news conference preceding Google's annual meeting, Schmidt, Page, and Brin talked about working together at Google. "The boys have grown up," Schmidt said, adding that they now functioned as senior executives with skills and experience. Later in the conference, Page mentioned that possessing fantastic wealth did have a benefit: "I don't have to do laundry."

Google's success transformed Page and Brin into public figures, and they guard their personal lives tightly. But there have been major changes for both since the days when they used to work through the night at the Google headquarters in Susan Wojcicki's garage.

Brin married Anne Wojcicki, Susan's younger sister, in 2007. The wedding was performed on a sandbar in the Bahamas; Wojcicki wore a white swimsuit and Brin a black one. The couple have one son, born in 2008.

Wojcicki graduated from Yale University with a B.S. in biology. She worked in health care investing for a decade before leaving to cofound 23andMe, a biotech company that provides personalized genetic mapping. Google is an investor in the company. Schmidt has stated publicly that Google was careful to ensure that the terms of the investment were all "by the book."

Brin had a personal reason to support genetic testing. His mother, Eugenia, had been diagnosed with Parkinson's disease, a nervous system disorder that affects muscle function. Genetic testing showed that Brin had above-average chances of developing Parkinson's due to a gene mutation. Brin believed that knowledge about

Brin and his wife, Anne Wojcicki, attend an event in New York City promoting Wojcicki's biotech company, 23andMe.

one's own genes can help people make informed decisions about their health.

Page also married in 2007. He and Lucinda (Lucy) Southworth, then a Ph.D. candidate, were married on a Caribbean island owned by British business tycoon Richard Branson. The couple have one son, born in 2009. Southworth has since completed her bioinformatics Ph.D.

Page and Brin have both received significant awards and recognition for their achievements. Both were awarded the prestigious Marconi Prize, given for innovations in information technology, in 2004. They have both been elected to the National Academy of Engineering, as has been Schmidt.

Green Google

In 2009, Google hired out a herd of two hundred goats to graze down a field of weeds. It was an entertaining sight—seeing goats grazing on the grounds of a powerful high-tech corporation—but the goats also represent one of Google's efforts in environmental sustainability, large and small. Google tries to minimize energy and water usage in its offices and encourages Googlers to make "low carbon" commutes to save energy. In the past, Google offered $5,000 incentives to employees who purchased hybrid vehicles; today, Googlers can drive a plug-in electrical vehicle in the GFleet, Google's car-sharing program. Google engineers work to incorporate green features in products and services. Google has also incorporated energy-saving practices in its data centers, which require a huge amount of electricity and water. The company disclosed its energy use figures in 2011: the amount of electricity it draws would power two hundred thousand homes. Data centers account for most of its electricity usage. Google pointed out that 25 percent of its energy came from renewable sources. Google.org, Google's philanthropic arm, supports environmental initiatives. The company has invested substantially in renewable energy projects such as a wind farms.

Both Page and Brin have invested in Tesla Motors, an electric vehicle company. They also acquired a 767 jet in 2005, and have since added several more planes to their fleet. The planes are kept at NASA's Moffat Field, which is close to the Googleplex. As a condition for allowing the use of the airport, NASA gets to equip the planes with scientific instruments and use them for research. Page is a trustee on the board of the X-PRIZE, which awards innovators in various fields. Brin has invested in Space Adventures, which may someday launch him on a trip as a space tourist.

Schmidt remained active in politics, business, and philanthropy during his time at Google. He supported Barack Obama's presidential campaign in 2008 and served on his transition team after his election as president. Also in 2008, Schmidt actively opposed Proposition 8, the ballot issue that banned gay marriage. He held a seat on Apple's board of directors from 2006 until 2009, when Google's development of Android created an irreconcilable conflict of interest. He was also named chair of the New America Foundation, a think tank, in 2008. Schmidt and his wife, Wendy, established the Eric Schmidt Family Foundation in 2006 to support research in energy and sustainability. Schmidt is also an avid jet pilot. He has also cowritten the upcoming book *Empire of the Mind: The Dawn of the Techno-Political Age*, which examines the role of technology in promoting democracy.

AN ESTABLISHED COMPANY

Google has grown up as well. It is now a major company with 24,400 employees around the world. In 2010, international revenue made up more than half of its total revenue.

The year 2008 marked Google's tenth birthday. It had become a respected company that had traveled far from its roots as a start-up. Some observers have hinted that Google is starting to lose its googliness—management and corporate conventions are beginning to stifle the innovative spirit that brought about its success. Many of Google's top personnel have been with the company from the early days, but employee retention has become an issue. Some engineers, frustrated with Google's bureaucratic process, have left to work for younger companies, such as Facebook, or form their own start-ups.

The case of Google Video contrasted with YouTube provides an example. Google Video, which was carefully monitored by Google's lawyers and executives during development, lacked the ambitious vision of YouTube, which was created more spontaneously and intuitively.

By this time, Google was well experienced with legal entanglements. Google hired David Drummond as the company's chief legal officer in 2002. The company's first major lawsuit began that same year, when Overture sued Google for patent infringement. Since then, Google has fought legal challenges both trivial

On September 21, 2011, Schmidt consults with Google's chief legal officer David Drummond (*right*) while testifying before a U.S. Senate panel on "The Power of Google: Serving Consumers or Threatening Competition?" in Washington, D.C.

and significant. Its legal department has grown to more than three hundred employees. One of Google's biggest legal challenges concerned its 2007 acquisition of DoubleClick, an online ad serving company. With a price of $3.1 billion, it became Google's biggest acquisition. The Federal Trade Commission (FTC) launched an antitrust investigation over the deal, but it eventually ruled that the acquisition was not anticompetitive and could continue. In 2008, the DOJ threatened to launch yet another antitrust violation investigation, this time combined with the charge of attempted monopolization. This time, the deal at stake was a proposed acquisition of Yahoo! by Google. Google halted the acquisition rather than fight the DOJ. As Google has grown and expanded, it has become the target of numerous antitrust inquiries in recent years in Europe and Asia, as well as in the United States. In September 2011, Schmidt testified before a U.S. Senate panel about Google's search result rankings and business practices.

The 2008 economic recession affected Google and slowed its rate of growth. Hiring tapered down, and some of Google's ten thousand contract workers were laid off. The value of Google stocks declined. Some of the perks were trimmed. Most were minor, such as the elimination of bottled water and a cutback in some food costs. One change that caused an outcry among employees was the steep hike in cost for day care. Nevertheless, Google survived and even thrived as the recession turned to recovery. In the company's 2009 press release, Schmidt reported healthy revenue growth and stated that considering the economic circumstances, "this was an extraordinary end to the year."

LOOKING AHEAD

Google welcomed Page back to the position of CEO on April 4, 2011. Although there were no formal public announcements concerning Page's immediate vision for the company, he quickly went to work reorganizing Google's management structure. He trimmed the bureaucracy, eliminated some projects, and redefined Google's focus. Page has put a fresh emphasis on quick decision-making, which had been difficult to achieve with three company leaders weighing in on important issues.

One of the company's new top priorities was social media. Facebook had come to dominate social networking. Google had released social products and services in the past, such as Orkut, Google Wave, and Google Buzz, but none of these gained a substantial following. Rumors emerged that the new social project was so important that a substantial portion of employee bonuses would be dependent on the outcome. In June 2011, Google launched Google+ as a direct challenge to Facebook—a company that does not feature Google ads on its site.

Two months later, Google announced its biggest deal ever: the $12.5 billion acquisition of Motorola Mobility Holdings. The mobile device maker brought with it thousands of patents, as well as a range of products. The deal increased Google's clout in the mobile computing industry. Google also announced its $125 million acquisition of Zagat in September. The restaurant review service has the potential to enhance Google Places, the company's site for local business listings.

In November 2011, Google announced that it was modifying its music service, including the introduction of a new store, Google Music. The service sells individual tracks and albums, and enables customers to store the music on cloud accounts. Google Music gives Android users expanded options for managing their music and promotes Google+ by allowing users to share music with friends. The new product competes with other music services, such as Apple's iTunes, Amazon MP3, and Spotify.

What does the future hold for Google, led by Larry Page? If Google succeeds in its quest to foster innovation, this is impossible to predict. Google will continue to develop projects in cloud computing. It will vigorously promote Google+, which received favorable reviews soon after it was announced. It will put its Motorola acquisition to good use. Brin, meanwhile, has redirected his focus toward speculative projects, many of them involving robotics, in a secret lab called "Google X" that might yield the company's next big breakthrough. But Google currently faces stiff competition from other tech companies, such as Apple and Facebook. As one of the most powerful tech companies, Google is in a position where it must defend its dominance, even as it looks ahead to new innovations.

SERGEY BRIN, LARRY PAGE, AND ERIC SCHMIDT

SERGEY BRIN

Born: August 21, 1973, in Moscow, Russia

Education: M.S., Stanford University; B.A./B.S., University of Maryland

Current Residence: San Francisco, California

Marital Status: Married to Anne Wojcicki

Children: 1

Job Title (2011–): Cofounder

Career History: Google President, 1998–2001; Google President of Technology, 2001–2011

Net Worth: $19.8 billion [March 2011; *Forbes*]

LARRY PAGE

Born: March 26, 1973, in East Lansing, Michigan

Education: M.S., Stanford University; B.A./B.S., University of Michigan

Current Residence: Palo Alto, California

Marital Status: Married to Lucinda Southworth

Children: 1

Job Title (2011–): CEO

Career History: Google CEO, 1998–2001; Google

President of Products, 2001–2011

Net Worth: $19.8 billion [March 2011; *Forbes*]

ERIC SCHMIDT

Born: April 27, 1955, in Falls Church, Virginia

Education: Ph.D., University of California, Berkeley; M.S., University of California, Berkeley; B.A./B.S., Princeton University;

Current Residence: Atherton, California

Marital Status: Married to Wendy Schmidt

Children: 2

Job Title (2011–): Executive Chairman

Career History: Researcher at Xerox PARC, 1982–1983; various positions at Sun Microsystems, 1983–1997; Novell CEO, 1997–2001; Google CEO, 2001–2011

Net Worth: $7 billion [March 2011; *Forbes*]

Fact Sheet on
GOOGLE INC.

Company Headquarters: 1600 Amphitheatre Parkway, Mountain View, California, 94043

Mission: To organize the worlds' information and make it universally accessible and useful.

Operation: Google is a global technology leader focused on improving the ways people connect with information.

Specialties: Search, ads, mobile, Android, online video

CEO: Larry Page

Founders: Larry Page and Sergey Brin

Area Served: Worldwide

Incorporated: September 4, 1998, in Menlo Park, California

Went Public: August 19, 2004

Opening Stock Price: $85/share

Stock Price All-Time High: $741.79 on November 7, 2007

Current Stock Price: $600.18 (November 17, 2011)

Stockholder's Meeting: Annually in May or June

Stock Ticker: GOOG on the NASDAQ Stock Market LLC

Annual Revenue: $29.3 billion

Profits: $8.5 billion

Revenue from Advertising: $28.2 billion

Net Worth: $190 billion

Number of Employees: 24,400 (in 2010)

1955 Eric Schmidt is born on April 27 in Falls Church, Virginia.

1973 Larry Page is born on March 26 in East Lansing, Michigan.

1973 Sergey Brin is born on August 21 in Moscow, USSR.

1982 Schmidt earns his Ph.D. at the University of California, Berkeley.

1993 Brin enrolls in Stanford University's computer science Ph.D. program

1995 Page enrolls in Stanford's computer science Ph.D. program; Page and Brin become friends and collaborators.

1996 Page and Brin launch a search engine called BackRub.

1997 Page and Brin register the domain name google.com; Google begins running at google.stanford.edu.

1998 Page and Brin publish, "The Anatomy of a Large-Scale Hypertextual Web Search Engine"; they raise $1 million from investors for their company; Google, Inc., is incorporated in September; Page and Brin rent a garage for Google's headquarters.

1999 Google raises $25 million from venture capitalists;

it hires Charlie Ayers as company chef; AdWords is launched.

2000 Google becomes Yahoo!'s search provider.

2001 Schmidt is hired as Google's CEO.

2002 AdWords Select is introduced and replaces the early version of AdWords; Google announces that it will provide search and ad services for AOL; Google News is launched.

2003 Google acquires Pyra Labs, creator of Blogger; AdSense is launched; Google Print is launched.

2004 Google relocates to the current Googleplex in Mountain View; Gmail is launched; a well-known magazine prints an article about Page and Brin that violates the "quiet period" in Google's IPO process; Google goes public with its IPO; it announces that it will begin scanning books of many prestigious libraries as part of Google Book Search.

2005 Google Maps is launched; Google acquires Android; publishers and authors sue Google over digitizing books for Google Book Search.

2006 google.cn begins operating in China; Google's first data center begins operation in Oregon; Schmidt joins Apple's board of directors; Google acquires YouTube; Google Docs is launched.

2007 *Fortune* names Google the country's best company

to work for; Viacom sues Google for copyright infringement on YouTube; Google announces the acquisition of DoubleClick, an online ad servicing company; Street View is launched as a feature of Google Maps; the Android platform is launched.

2008 Google launches Chrome, its Web browser; a settlement is reached over Google Book Search.

2009 Hackers break into Google's system and steal information on Chinese activists.

2010 Google announces that it will no longer censor search results on google.cn; Google purchases flight-data maker ITA; it wins in the Viacom lawsuit case; Google Instant is launched on the Google search engine.

2011 The Google Book Search settlement is rejected in court; Page replaces Schmidt as CEO; Google launches Google+; it acquires Motorola Mobile Holdings, Inc.; it buys the restaurant review service Zagat; it launches new search tool Google Flight Search; Google Music is introduced.

Glossary

acquisition The obtaining of ownership or a controlling interest in a company.

afflict To cause great physical or mental pain.

algorithm A step-by-step set of rules for solving a problem, especially in mathematics or computing.

amenity A feature that provides comfort, convenience, or enjoyment.

anticompetitive Tending to reduce or discourage fair competition, especially in business.

anti-Semitism Discrimination against or hostility toward Jews.

antitrust Regulating or opposing trusts and other business monopolies, especially in order to promote fair competition.

artificial intelligence The subfield of computer science dealing with the study and design of machines that simulate human intelligence.

authoritarian Expecting unquestioning obedience, as a government.

bar mitzvah The religious ceremony of a Jewish boy who has reached the age of thirteen and is believed to be ready to observe religious principles and take part in public worship.

beta test A test of a computer product conducted

before the product is released commercially.

bioinformatics The branch of information science that uses computers, mathematics, and theory to model and analyze biological systems, particularly those involving genetic material.

bureaucracy The management or administration of a large or complex organization, especially one characterized by excessive observance of rules and routine.

campus The grounds and buildings of a university or other institution.

censor To remove content, such as in books or movies, deemed inappropriate on moral, political, or other grounds.

click-through rate The percentage of viewers of an online ad who click on the ad.

computer science The branch of engineering that deals with computer hardware and software.

copyright The exclusive right to control intellectual property, such as a book or piece of music, for a certain period of time.

database An organized set of data in a computer system that can be easily searched and updated.

digitize To convert data, such as images, to digital form.

doctorate Also known as doctor of philosophy (Ph.D.); the highest academic degree granted by a university.

domain A Web site's address on the Internet.

dot-com bubble The stock market bubble that inflated the value of Internet firms in the late 1990s; many of these collapsed when the bubble popped in 2001.

entrepreneur An individual who organizes and operates a business, especially one that involves a financial risk.

executive A high-level business manager.

exuberant Extremely enthusiastic in nature.

faculty The body of teachers in a college or university.

hypertext The way of joining a word or image to another page or document on the Internet or in another computer program so that a user can move easily from one to the other.

incorporate To include as a feature; also, to form a legal corporation.

infastructure The basic structure or features of a system or organization.

infringe To encroach upon so as to break a law or violate someone's rights.

initial public offering (IPO) A private company's first sale of stock to the public.

innovate To invent or introduce something new.

intellectual property A work or an invention that is the result of creativity, such as a design or manuscript, to which someone has rights and for which someone may apply for a patent, copyright, trademark, and so forth.

keyword A word used by a search engine to indicate the content of a Web site.

license To grant formal permission to enter or use the property of another, such as a patent or copyright.

logistics The handling of the practical details of an activity or operation.

management The executives or administrators who direct and operate a business or organization.

marketing The process of promoting a product or service to potential buyers.

monopoly Exclusive control of a product or service in a particular market by a single entity.

Montessori school A school following the educational system developed by Marie Montessori, which emphasizes self-guided learning.

obtrusive Overly prominent.

patent The legal right, granted by the government, to produce or sell an invention for a specific number of years.

philanthropy The practice of donating money to humanitarian causes.

platform The basic technology of a computer system's hardware and software, such as its operating system.

precursor A person or thing that precedes another.

proliferate To increase rapidly in number.

redundancy The use of words or data that could be omitted without loss of meaning or function; repetition of information.

regime A system of government, especially an authoritarian one.

revenue A company's income.

search engine A computer program that retrieves information from the Internet related to keywords entered by the user.

search engine optimization (SEO) The methods used to raise a Web site's ranking in search engine results in an attempt to attract more traffic.

shareholder One who owns shares of stock, especially in a corporation.

sustainability The capability of being continued or maintained with little long-term effect on the environment.

thesis A piece of writing based on original research submitted by a candidate for a university degree.

venture capitalist A private investor or investment firm that provides money to a new or expanding company, often high-tech, with the expectation of a high return due to high risk.

visa An official document or endorsement on a passport that indicates that the bearer may enter or leave a particular country.

Web traffic The number of visitors to a Web site.

For More Information

Apple Inc.

1 Infinite Loop

Cupertino, CA 95014

(408) 996-1010

Web site: http://www.apple.com

This tech giant produces computers, electronic devices, and
software.

Canadian Trade Commissioner Service

TCS Enquiries Service

Foreign Affairs and International Trade Canada

125 Sussex Drive

Ottawa, ON K1A 0G2

Canada

(888) 306-9991

Web site: http://www.tradecommissioner.gc.ca

This service helps companies flourish on a global level while
lowering the cost of doing business throughout the world.

Electronic Frontier Foundation
454 Shotwell Street
San Francisco CA 94110
(415) 436-9333
Web site: http://www.eff.org
The Electronic Frontier Foundation is a group with the goal
of supporting Internet rights and freedoms.

Entrepreneurs' Organization
500 Montgomery Street
Alexandria, VA 22314
(703) 519-6700
Web site: http://www.eonetwork.org
The Entrepreneurs' Organization presents members
    with information about starting a small business and
    offers networking and educational opportunities.

Facebook
1601 Willow Road and Bayfront Expressway
Menlo Park, CA 94025
Web site: http://www.facebook.com
This is the world's leading social networking service.

Google Inc.
1600 Amphitheatre Parkway

Mountain View, CA 94043

(650) 253-0000

Web site: http://www.google.com

A tech company, Google is best known for its search engine.

Google Toronto

10 Dundas Street East, Suite 600

Toronto, ON M5B 2G9

Canada

(416) 915-8200

Web site: http://www.google.ca

The Toronto office is just one of the Canadian contacts for Google products in Canada; there are also offices in Montréal and Waterloo.

Internet Society

1775 Wiehle Avenue, Suite 201

Reston, VA 20190-510

(703) 439-2120

Web site: http://www.isoc.org

This organization works to address issues relating to the Internet, including Internet education, standards, and policy.

Media Awareness Network

1500 Merivale Road, 3rd floor

Ottawa, ON K2E 6Z5

Canada

(613) 224-7721

Web site: http://www.media-awareness.ca

The Web site for this network contains a selection of digital
literacy resources for students, teachers, and parents.

National Science Foundation

4201 Wilson Boulevard

Arlington, VA 22230

(703) 292-5111

Web site: http://www.nsf.gov

This government agency funds scientific research in a
variety of fields.

Stanford University

450 Serra Mall

Stanford, CA 94305

(650) 723-2300

Web site: http://www.stanford.edu

Stanford is one of the world's preeminent research and
teaching institutions. Its Computer Science Department is part of the School of Engineering.

TechAmerica Foundation

601 Pennsylvania Avenue NW

North Building, Suite 600

Washington, DC 20004

(202) 682-9110

Web site: http://www.techamerica.org

TechAmerica is the leading trade association for the American technology industry. It provides a wide range of professional development opportunities for its members.

Tesla Motors

3500 Deer Creek

Palo Alto, CA 94304

(650) 681-5000

Web site: http://www.teslamotors.com

An electric vehicle company, Tesla was founded in 2003 by a group of Silicon Valley engineers.

U.S. Association for Small Business and Entrepreneurship (USASBE)

Belmont University

1900 Belmont Boulevard

Nashville, TN 37212

(615) 460-2615

Web site: http://www.usasbe.org

The USASBE fosters advancement in the four pillars of small business and entrepreneurship: education, research, outreach, and public policy. Its mission is to foster the creation of new for-profit and social ventures.

University of California, Berkeley
Electrical Engineering and Computer Science, College of Engineering
387 Soda Hall
Berkeley, CA 94720-1776
(510) 642-1042
Web site: http://www.eecs.berkeley.edu
Berkeley's Department of Electrical Engineering and Computer Science is world renowned and offers research and instructional study programs in engineering and computer science.

Wired.com
Web site: http://www.wired.com
This is a daily technology news Web site that is the digital home of the monthly *Wired* magazine.

X Prize Foundation
5510 Lincoln Boulevard, Suite 100
Playa Vista, CA 90094-2034
(310) 741-4880
Web site: http://www.xprizefoundation.com

A nonprofit organization, the foundation offers prizes for breakthroughs in various fields.

Yahoo! Inc.
701 First Avenue
Sunnyvale, CA 94089
(408) 349-3300
Web site: http://www.yahoo.com
A tech company, Yahoo! developed from a Web directory project.

YouTube, LLC
901 Cherry Avenue
San Bruno, CA 94066
(650) 253-0000
Web site: http://www.youtube.com
YouTube, a video sharing site, is owned by Google.

WEB SITES

Due to the changing nature of Internet links, Rosen Publishing has developed an online list of Web sites related to the subject of this book. This site is updated regularly. Please use this link to access the list:

http://www.rosenlinks.com/ibio/google

For Further Reading

Ayers, Charlie. *Food 2.0: Secrets from the Chef Who Fed Google*. New York, NY: DK, 2008.

Brockman, John, ed. *Is the Internet Changing the Way You Think? The Net's Impact on Our Minds and Future*. New York, NY: Harper Perennial, 2011.

Carr, Nicholas. *The Big Switch: Rewiring the World, from Edison to Google*. New York, NY: W. W. Norton & Co., 2009.

Casnocha, Ben. *My Start-Up Life*. San Francisco, CA: Jossey-Bass, 2007.

Cohen, David, and Brad Feld. *Do More Faster: TechStars Lessons to Accelerate Your Startup*. Hoboken, NJ: Wiley, 2011.

Dougherty, Terri. *Freedom of Expression and the Internet*. Farmington Hills, MI: Lucent Books, 2010.

Draper, William H. *The Startup Game: Inside the Partnership Between Venture Capitalists and Entrepreneurs*. New York, NY: Palgrave Macmillan, 2011.

Friedman, Lauri S. *The Internet*. Farmington Hills, MI: Greenhaven Press, 2007.

Gaines, Ann Graham. *Ace Your Internet Research* (Ace It! Information Literacy). Berkeley Heights, NJ: Enslow Publishers, 2009.

Gilbert, Gilbert. *The Story of Google*. Mankato, MN: Creative Education, 2009.

Goldman, Aaron. *Everything I Know About Marketing I Learned from Google*. New York, NY: McGraw-Hill, 2011.

Hamen, Susan E. *Google: The Company and Its Founders*. Edina, MN: ABDO Publishing, 2011.

Henders, Harry. *Larry Page and Sergey Brin: Information at Your Fingertips* (Trailblazers in Science and Technology). New York, NY: Chelsea House Publishers, 2012.

Jarvis, Jeff. *What Would Google Do?* New York, NY: Collins Business, 2009.

Kallen, Stuart A. *The Information Revolution*. Farmington Hills, MI: Lucent Books, 2010.

Kirkpatrick, David. *The Facebook Effect: The Inside Story of the Company That Is Connecting the World*. New York, NY: Simon & Schuster, 2010.

Livingston, Jessica. *Founders at Work: Stories of Startups' Early Days*. Berkeley, CA: Apress, 2008.

McDowell, Gayle Laakmann. *The Google Resume: How to Prepare for a Career and Land a Job at Apple, Microsoft, Google, or Any Top Tech Company*. Hoboken, NJ: Wiley, 2011.

McPherson, Stephanie Sammartino. *Sergey Brin and Larry Page: Founders of Google* (USA Today Lifeline Biographies). Minneapolis, MN: Twenty-First Century Books, 2010.

Merrill, Douglas, and James A. Martin. *Getting Organized in the Google Era: How to Get Stuff Out of Your Head, Find It When You Need It, and Get It Done Right.* New York, NY: Broadway Books, 2010.

Miller, Michael. *Googlepedia: The Ultimate Google Resource.* Indianapolis, IN: Que, 2009.

Parks, Peggy J. *Computer Hacking.* Farmington Hills, MI: Lucent Books, 2008.

Porterfield, Jason. *Conducting Basic and Advanced Searches* (Digital and Information Literacy). New York, NY: Rosen Publishing Group, 2010.

Raju, Jagmohan. *Smart Pricing: How Google, Priceline, and Leading Businesses Use Pricing Innovation for Profitability.* Upper Saddle River, NJ: Pearson Prentice Hall, 2010.

Rothwell, William J., John Lindholm, and William G. Wallick. *What CEOs Expect from Corporate Training: Building Workplace Learning and Performance Initiatives That Advance Organizational Goals.* New York, NY: AMACOM, 2003.

Sapet, Kerrily. *Google Founders: Larry Page and Sergey Brin.* Greensboro, NC: Morgan Reynolds Publishing, 2011.

Stewart, Gail B. *Larry Page and Sergey Brin: The Google Guys*. San Diego, CA: KidHaven Press, 2007.

Vance, Ashlee. *Geek Silicon Valley: The Inside Guide to Palo Alto, Stanford, Menlo Park, Mountain View, Santa Clara, Sunnyvale, San Jose, San Francisco*. Guilford, CT: Globe Pequot, 2007.

White, Casey. *Sergey Brin and Larry Page: The Founders of Google* (Internet Career Biographies). New York, NY: Rosen Publishing Group, 2007.

Witten, Ian, Marco Gori, and Teresa Numerico. *Web Dragons: Inside the Myths of Search Engine Technology*. San Francisco, CA: Morgan Kaufmann, 2006.

Yahoo!, ed. *The Yahoo! Style Guide: The Ultimate Sourcebook for Writing, Editing, and Creating Content for the Digital World*. New York, NY: St. Martin's Griffin, 2010.

Bibliography

Ahmed, Kamal. "Google's Eric Schmidt Predicts the Future of Computing—and He Plans to Be Involved." *Telegraph*, February 5, 2011. Retrieved September 9, 2011(http://www.telegraph.co.uk/technology/google/8303847/Googles-Eric-Schmidt-predicts-the-future-of-computing-and-he-plans-to-be-involved.html).

Auletta, Ken. *Googled: The End of the World as We Know It. New York*, NY: Penguin Press, 2009.

Austin, Scott. "Google Lost Groupon, But Still Tops Most-Active Acquirer List." *Wall Street Journal*, January 4, 2011. Retrieved September 9, 2011 (http://blogs.wsj.com/venturecapital/2011/01/04/google-lost-groupon-but-still-tops-most-active-acquirer-list).

Batelle, John. *The Search: How Google and Its Rivals Rewrote the Rules of Business and Transformed Our Culture*. New York, NY: Portfolio, 2005.

"The Boys Have Grown Up." Guardian.co.uk, May 9, 2008. Retrieved September 8, 2011 (http://www.guardian.co.uk/business/2008/may/09/google.google).

Brandt, Richard L. *Inside Larry & Sergey's Brain*. New York, NY: Portfolio, 2009.

Brin, Sergey. "A Library to Last Forever." *New York Times*, October 9, 2009.

Dvorak, John C. "Eric Schmidt, Google and Privacy." *Market Watch*, December 11, 2009. Retrieved September 7, 2011 (http://www.marketwatch.com /story/eric-schmidt-google-and-privacy-2009-12-11).

Edmonston, Peter. "Dealbook: Google's I.P.O., Five Years Later." *New York Times*, August 19, 2009. Retrieved September 6, 2011(http://dealbook.nytimes .com/2009/08/19/googles-ipo-5-years-later).

Edwards, Douglas. *I'm Feeling Lucky: The Confessions of Google Employee Number 59*. Boston, MA: Houghton Mifflin Harcourt, 2011.

Efrati, Amir. "For Google CEO Larry Page, a Difficult Premiere Role." *Wall Street Journal*, August 30, 2011. Retrieved September 5, 2011(http://online.wsj.com/ article/SB1000142405311190335270457653652198458 62128.html).

"Enlightenment Man." *Economist*, December 4, 2008. Retrieved September 4, 2011 (http://www.economist .com/node/12673407?story_id=12673407).

Girard, Bernard. *The Google Way: How One Company Is Revolutionizing Management as We Know It*. San Francisco, CA: No Starch Press, 2009.

Glanz, James. "Google Details, and Defends, Its Use of Electricity." *New York Times*, September 8, 2011.

"Google Announces Fourth Quarter and Fiscal Year 2010 Results and Management Changes." Google Investor Relations, January 20, 2011. Retrieved September 5,

2011(http://investor.google.com/earnings/2010
/Q4_google_earnings.html).

Hafner, Katie. "Silicon Valley Wide-Eyed Over a Bride."
New York Times, May 29, 2007. Retrieved September
1, 2011 (http://www.nytimes.com/2007/05/29
/technology/29google.html).

Helft, Miguel. "Federal Judge Rejects Google's Negotiated
Deal to Digitize Books." *New York Times*,
March 23, 2011.

Krieger, Lisa M. "Stanford Earns $336 Million Off
Google Stock." *San Jose Mercury News*, December
1, 2005. Retrieved September 1, 2011 (http://
www.redorbit.com/news/education/318480/
stanford_earns_336_million_off_google_stock).

"Larry Page." *Michigan Engineer*, Spring/Summer 2001.
Retrieved September 2, 2011 (https://www.eecs
.umich.edu/eecs/alumni/Stories/Page_coe_me.html).

Levy, Steven. *In the Plex: How Google Thinks, Works, and
Shapes Our Lives*. New York, NY:
Simon & Schuster, 2011.

Levy, Steven. "The Larry Page Re-Org: Google
Kremlinology." *Wired*, April 12, 2011.
Retrieved September 9, 2011 (http://
www.wired.com/epicenter/2011/04/
the-larry-page-re-org-google-kremlinology).

Lowe, Janet. *Google Speaks: Secrets of the World's Greatest
Billionaire Entrepreneurs, Sergey Brin and Larry Page*.

Hoboken, NJ: Wiley, 2009.

Malseed, Mark. "The Story of Sergey Brin." *Moment*, February 2007. Retrieved September 8, 2011 (http://www.momentmag.com/Exclusive/2007/02/200702-BrinFeature.html).

Scott, Virginia. *Corporations That Changed the World: Google*. Westport, CT: Greenwood Press, 2008.

Sisario, Ben. "Music Service from Google Will Sell and Store Songs." *New York Times*, November 17, 2011.

Stross, Randall. *Planet Google: One Company's Audacious Plan to Organize Everything We Know*. New York, NY: Free Press, 2008.

Vaidhyanathan, Siva. *The Googlization of Everything: (and Why We Should Worry)*. Berkeley, CA: University of California Press, 2011.

Vise, David A., and Mark Malseed. *The Google Story: Inside the Hottest Business, Media, and Technology Success of Our Time*. New York, NY: Delta Trade Paperbacks, 2008.

Index

A

AdSense, 59, 64
AdWords, 54, 57–58
AdWords Select, 58
AltaVista, 25, 31, 36
America Online, 48, 61
"Anatomy of a Large-Scale Hypertextual Web Search Engine, The," 31
Android, 6, 36, 72, 79, 83, 93, 98
Apple, 36, 83, 93, 98
April Fool's Day, tradition of pranks on, 64, 68, 73
Ask Jeeves, 61
Auletta, Ken, 23
Ayers, Charlie, 76

B

BackRub, 28, 29, 33
Bechtolsheim, Andy, 32–33
Bezos, Jeff, 33
Bharat, Krishna, 44–45, 62, 77
Blogger, 6, 66
Brin, Sergey
    childhood and early education of, 10, 11–15
    marriage and family of, 90
    at Stanford, 21–33
    and starting up Google, 34–48

C

Campbell, Bill, 61
Cheriton, David, 32
Cutts, Matt, 45–46

D

Doerr, John, 47, 50, 51, 55, 61
DoubleClick, 95
Drummond, David, 94

E

Earthlink, 61
Empire of the Mind: The Dawn of the Techno-Political Age, 93
Excite, 24, 30–31, 36

F

Facebook, 36, 97, 98

G

Garcia-Molina, Hector, 25
Gates, Bill, 22
Gmail, 6, 64, 77, 81

Google
    ads and profitability, 56–59
    in China, 86–87
    and controversy/legal chal-
        lenges, 9, 63, 64, 80–81,
        82, 84–85, 94–96
    and environmental sustain-
        ability, 92
    hiring practices of, 41, 46, 74
    and initial public offering,
        65–70
    naming of, 29
    philosophy of, 8, 38, 54
    work environment/benefits, 8,
        34–35, 42, 65, 74–77, 96
Google+, 36, 97, 98
Google Books, 79, 84–85
Google Chrome, 36, 71, 79
Googled, 23
Google Docs, 81
Google Doodles, 43
Google Earth, 81
Google Flight Search, 78
Google Instant, 40
Google Local, 66
Google Maps, 6, 66, 79–81, 87
Google Music, 98
Google News, 6, 44, 62–63, 77
Google.org, 71, 92
Google Places, 97
Googleplex, 8, 34, 63–65, 74–76,
        82, 93
Google Product Search, 60
Google Scholar, 60
Google Videos, 60, 82, 94

GoTo (Overture), 36, 57–58,
    61, 94

H

Hölzle, Urs, 44

I

Image Search, 60
Inktomi, 24, 36, 49, 61

J

Jobs, Steve, 50, 83

K

Kamangar, Salar, 44, 46, 82
Kleiner Perkins Caufield, 47–48
Kordestani, Omar, 46

M

Marconi Prize, 91
Mayer, Marissa, 44
Moritz, Mike, 47, 50, 61
Motorola Mobility Holdings,
    97, 98
Motwani, Rajeev, 25

N

National Academy of Engineer-
    ing, 92
Netscape, 48

O

Overture (GoTo), 36, 57–58,
    61, 94

P

Page, Larry
 childhood and early
  education of, 10, 16, 17–20
 marriage and family of, 91
 at Stanford, 16, 21–33
 and starting up Google,
  34–48
PageRank, 27–28, 30, 33, 37
Patel, Amit, 60

R

Reese, Jim, 45

S

SafeSearch, 40
Schmidt, Mike
 childhood and education of,
  52–53
 early career of, 53–55
search engines, early, 24–25, 36
Sequoia Capital, 47–48
Silverstein, Craig, 34

Space Adventures, 93

T

Tesla, Nikola, 16
Tesla Motors, 93

W

Winograd, Terry, 23, 25, 48
Wojcicki, Anne, 90
Wojcicki, Susan, 34, 44,
  75–76, 90

X

X-PRIZE, 93

Y

Yahoo!, 18, 21, 25, 31, 36, 47,
  49–50, 96
YouTube, 6, 71, 73, 79, 82, 94

Z

Zagat, 97

ABOUT THE AUTHOR

Corona Brezina is an author who has written numerous books for young adults. Some of her previous books have focused on technology and current affairs, including *Careers in Nanotechnology* and several volumes in the Real World Economics series. She lives in Chicago, Illinois.

PHOTO CREDITS